George Brace Loomis

The Progressive Glee and Chorus Book

George Brace Loomis

The Progressive Glee and Chorus Book

ISBN/EAN: 9783337348977

Printed in Europe, USA, Canada, Australia, Japan

Cover: Foto ©Thomas Meinert / pixelio.de

More available books at **www.hansebooks.com**

THE

PROGRESSIVE

GLEE AND CHORUS BOOK;

CONSISTING CHIEFLY OF MUSIC SELECTED FROM THE

BEST GERMAN, ENGLISH, AND ITALIAN AUTHORS:

HANDEL,	*HAYDN,*	*BEETHOVEN,*	*MOZART,*	*MENDELSSOHN,*	*WEBER,*
SCHUMANN,	*SCHUBERT,*	*MARSCHNER,*	*ABT,*	*FRANZ,*	*KREUTZER.*
CURSCHMANN,	*BARNBY,*	*HATTON,*	*FARMER,*	*COSTA,*	*RICHARDS,*
GLOVER.	*BELLINI,*	*VERDI,*	*DONIZETTI,*	*MEYERBEER,*	*FLOTOW*

AND MANY OTHERS.

ADAPTED FOR USE IN

HIGH SCHOOLS, ADVANCED SINGING CLASSES, AND MUSICAL SOCIETIES.

ARRANGED AND COMPOSED BY

GEORGE B. LOOMIS.

DESIGNED TO FOLLOW

LOOMIS'S PROGRESSIVE MUSIC LESSON SERIES.

IVISON, BLAKEMAN, TAYLOR & CO.,
NEW YORK AND CHICAGO.

COPYRIGHT, 1879, BY IVISON, BLAKEMAN, TAYLOR & CO.

PREFACE.

THIS Book is designed, primarily, to complete the Series known as "LOOMIS' PROGRESSIVE MUSIC LESSONS," it being the fifth book.

While the series aims to present the subject in such a progressive manner as to adapt it especially to the needs of graded schools, from Primary to Grammar and High School grades, No. 4 is equally well adapted, apart from the series, as a song book for Female Seminaries and private schools, where two and three-part music is desired. This last book is also well adapted for use in advanced singing classes and singing societies, where a good class of music is desired, which shall be of moderate difficulty and of sufficient merit to be worth learning.

Some of the features of this book, to which attention is directed, are *first*, its *elementary* department, in which the elements of music are presented in a concise and comprehensive form, to which are added some new features, as the names and compass of different kinds of voices and instruments, a classification of collections of voices and instruments, a list of different kinds of instruments used in orchestras and bands, names of different classes of musical compositions, etc. Then follows a brief treatise on harmony and brief biographical sketches of a few of the great composers, and a few choice solfeggios and oratorio solos for class practice. It is believed that this portion of the book is somewhat more educational in its make-up than books of this class generally.

The musical portion of the work consists of three and four-part secular and sacred music, composed, selected, and arranged from many sources, largely from the German and English, of that which seemed to the author to be adapted to the end in view—that of educating the people through the medium of song. Of the power of music in this direction we have yet much to learn. Germany appreciates it; England is following in her wake; and may we not hope that our own favored America may soon be abreast of them in this regard, so that it may be possible, in every village and hamlet of our land, to find some who, on many a social occasion, may be able to form a chorus, and sing many popular songs, the words and music of which are worthy to be woven into the warp and woof of our American character.

Many of the songs of this book have been translated and arranged especially for it, and it is believed that they are of a character which shall commend them to those who desire to go beyond that which is merely superficial and transitory.

The pieces are arranged as nearly in progressive order as the best arrangement of pages would permit.

If the book shall contribute in any degree to building up and establishing in the rising generation greater purity and moral integrity, a truer and nobler manhood, the work of the author shall not have been in vain. To have contributed to such an end will compensate for the labor expended which has been a labor of love.

GEO. B. LOOMIS.

INDIANAPOLIS, IND., December, 1878.

THE ELEMENTS OF MUSIC

PRESENTED

IN THE FORM OF STATEMENTS.

CHAPTER I.

NOTE.—In the first four books of this series, the subject was so presented in its elements, practically and theoretically, as to need here little more, if anything, than brief statements on each topic, followed, when necessary, with such explanations or illustrations as may seem needful to enable new pupils to obtain a correct idea of things, technical terms, definitions, signs, etc., employed in music.

Statement 1. Musical sounds are called tones.

Statement 2. Tones have four properties or attributes: Length or Duration, Pitch, Force or Power, and Quality.

NOTE.—To be able to interpret readily and correctly in song or upon an instrument the symbols or signs employed to represent these different properties, constitutes one a good reader of music.

Statement 3. In treating of these tone-properties, three departments are necessary.
Whatever pertains in any way to tone-**lengths** belongs to the department of **Rhythmics**.

Statement 4. Whatever pertains in any way to tone-**pitch** belongs to the department of **Melodics**.

Statement 5. Whatever pertains in any way to tone-**force** or **quality** belongs to the department of **Dynamics**.

Statement 6. The **length** or duration of tones is represented chiefly by characters called notes, named whole (𝅝), half (𝅗𝅥), quarter (♩), eighth (♪), sixteenth (𝅘𝅥𝅯), etc.
Each note may be followed by a **dot**, which increases its time-value **one-half**, as, 𝅝. = 𝅝𝅗𝅥, 𝅗𝅥. = 𝅗𝅥♩, ♩. = ♩♪, etc.
Each note may be followed by **two dots**, which increase its time-value **three-fourths**, as, 𝅝.. = 𝅝𝅗𝅥♩, 𝅗𝅥.. = 𝅗𝅥♩♪, etc.

Statement 7. Characters indicating duration of silence are called **Rests**, named Whole (𝄻), Half (𝄼), Quarter (𝄽), Eighth (𝄾), Sixteenth (𝄿), etc. Rests are sometimes used as follows: , the first as long as **two** whole rests, the second as **four**, etc.
The whole rest is sometimes used to fill any kind of measure. Dots may follow **Rests**, as **Notes**, with like results.

Statement 8. Another character employed to represent length is the **Tie**, a curved line under or over two or more notes on the **same** degree of the staff, by which a single tone as long as the several notes indicate, is represented, as, .

THE ELEMENTS OF MUSIC.

Statement 9. Another character representing length is the **Slur**, like the Tie in form and use, save that the notes are on **different** degrees of the staff, as, ![slur] . With eighth and sixteenth notes the slur is indicated as follows: ![slur2] and ![slur3] , etc.

Statement 10. Still another character indicating a tone or rest of indefinite length, according to the fancy of the performer, is the **Pause or Hold**, made thus ⌒. It may be used over a **Note** or **Rest**.

Statement 11. The **Triplet** also is a representative of length, indicating that **three** notes with it have the same time-value as **two** notes of the same kind **without** it, as, 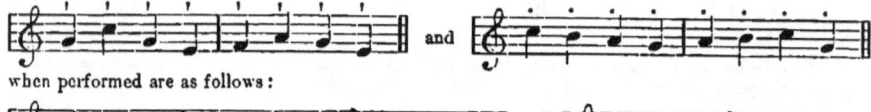, etc.

Statement 12. Points and dots over notes, called **Staccato** and **Marcato**, also have to do with the lengths of the tones, as,  when performed are as follows:

![music example] etc.

NOTE.—From the foregoing statements it appears that the representatives of tone-lengths are Notes primarily, and in connection with them are Dots, Tie, Slur, Pause or Hold, Triplet, Staccato and Marcato marks.

Statement 13. The relative length or duration of tones is computed or determined by portions of time, called **Measures**, of which there are four **kinds** in common use—double, triple, quadruple, and sextuple; or, two-part, three-part, four-part, and six-part.

Statement 14. Measures are represented by spaces between lines, called **Bars**, crossing the staff.

Statement 15. **Bars** are vertical lines crossing the staff, and used to separate written measures. A **Double Bar** is often used at the end of a line of poetry, or of a musical phrase, and always at the close of a piece of music.

Statement 16. Measures are indicated by **Counts** or **Beats**.

Statement 17. In double measure the beats are **down** and up; in triple measure, **down**, left, and up; in quadruple measure, **down**, left, **right**, and up; in sextuple measure, **down**, left, left, **right**, up, up, or, in **quick** movement, down and up.

Statement 18. The **first** part of each measure is **accented**, also the **third** part of quadruple and the **fourth** of sextuple measure, as indicated by heavy words in Statement 17.

Statement 19. A tone beginning with an **unaccented** part of a measure and continuing through the **accented** part, or with the last half of a part, and continuing through the first half of the next, is called a **Syncopated Tone**, and its representative, a **Syncopated Note**, as,

![music example]

Such a tone should receive **special accent**.

Statement 20. Since a tone one beat in length may be represented by different kinds of notes in different pieces of music, we have what is called **varieties** of measure; as, **half** variety, **quarter** variety, etc.

THE ELEMENTS OF MUSIC.

Statement 21. The **kind** of measure always depends upon the **number of beats in a measure**; as, two beats, double measure, etc.

Statement 22. The **variety** of measure depends upon the **kind of note to which we give one beat**; as, when a **half note** receives one beat, it is called **half variety**, etc.

Statement 23. The kind and variety of measure are usually indicated at the beginning of a piece of music by figures written in the form of a fraction, the **upper** figure indicating the **kind**, and the **lower** the **variety**, as follows:

Variety.	Kind. Double.	Kind. Triple.	Kind. Quadruple.	Kind. Sextuple.
Half.	₵ or 2/2 ♩ ♩	3/2 ♩ ♩ ♩	4/2 ♩ ♩ ♩ ♩	6/2 ♩ ♩ ♩ ♩ ♩ ♩
Quarter.	2/4 ♩ ♩	3/4 ♩ ♩ ♩	4/4 or 𝄴 ♩ ♩ ♩ ♩	6/4 ♩ ♩ ♩ ♩ ♩ ♩
Eighth.	2/8 ♪ ♪	3/8 ♪ ♪ ♪	4/8 ♪ ♪ ♪ ♪	6/8 ♪ ♪ ♪ ♪ ♪ ♪

Occasionally, measures are used marked $\frac{9}{8}$ and $\frac{12}{8}$, the formation of which will be readily understood from the table above, and are called **compound** forms of measure.

Statement 24. The word **time** is often used for **measure**; as, double **time**, triple time, etc. $\frac{2}{4}$ two-four time, $\frac{3}{8}$ three-eight time.

Statement 25. The figures indicating kind and variety of measure are sometimes called the **time-mark**, or **time-signature**.

Statement 26. The **time-value** of a note means the number of beats given to the tone it represents, and is determined by the **variety** of measure; as, in **half** variety of measure the time-value of a **half** note is **one** beat, in **quarter** variety, **two** beats, and in **eighth** variety, **four** beats.

Statement 27. When a portion of a piece of music is to be sung or played a **second time**, it may be indicated by some mark of repetition, of which there are three in common use; dots, D. C., and D. S.

Statement 28. When **dots** are used, their position determines how much is to be repeated; when D. C. is used, repeat from the beginning to the word **Fine**; when **D. S.** is used, repeat from a sign, 𝄋, or 𝄉, to **Fine**. **Fine** signifies **the end**.

NOTE.—The statements thus far relate only to tone-length.

Statement 29. By the **pitch** of tones is meant their **highness or lowness**.

Statement 30. Tones are named with respect to pitch either from their **relation** to other tones, or, **independent** of such relation.

Statement 31. That tone-pitch which is ascertained or determined by its **relation** to other tones is called **relative** pitch.

Statement 32. Relative pitch is named from the names of numbers, from one to eight, inclusive.

Statement 33. That tone-pitch which is independent of relation to other tones and is determined or ascertained by instrumental aid, is called **absolute** pitch.

THE ELEMENTS OF MUSIC.

Statement 34. Absolute pitch is named from the names of letters, A, B, C, D, E, F and G.

Statement 35. Eight tones arranged in a certain order of relative pitch are called the **Scale**, from Scala, meaning a **ladder**.

Statement 36. The tones of the scale are named relatively, one, two, three, four, five, six, seven, eight.

Eight of one scale becomes **one** of a higher scale, and **one** of one scale becomes **eight** of a lower scale.

Statement 37. The syllables commonly employed in singing the scale are Do, Re, Mi, Fa, Sol, La, Si, Do.

In the Italian method the syllables are used in place of the letters A, B, C, etc.

Statement 38. The pitch of tones is represented by the staff and clef. Each degree of the staff may be so modified by the use of a sharp, double-sharp, flat and double-flat as to represent five pitches, as follows:

NOTE.—The above statement differs somewhat from that often given, which is, that the staff **alone** represents pitch. If a staff is drawn, and it be asked, What pitch does a certain named degree represent? the answer is: It **may** represent **any** pitch, but **now** it represents **none**. Not until the **clef** is added does the staff represent definite pitch. The clef is the life-giving power.

Statement 39. Sharps and flats, when placed at the **beginning** of a piece of music, form, with the clef, the **Signature**; and when used **elsewhere** in the music, with the natural (♮) also, are called **Accidentals**.

Statement 40. The **Staff** consists of five parallel lines and four intermediate and two adjoining spaces, called **Degrees**. Short lines may be added above and below, called **Added** or **Leger** lines.

Statement 41. A **Clef** is a letter placed on some degree of the staff, giving it power to represent pitch, and by which we determine what pitch it and other degrees represent.

Statement 42. The word clef is from the French, and means **key**.

Statement 43. The letters which are used as **clefs** are G, F, and C, and in modern vocal music have **fixed positions** on the staff. In old English and orchestral music, the position of the C clef varies.

Statement 44. The position of G, as a clef, is the second line, of F is the fourth line, and of C is the third space. The shape and relative position of each is as follows:

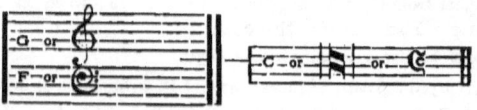

Statement 45. An **Interval** is the difference in pitch between two tones.

Statement 46. Intervals, when named from their **magnitude** or **size**, are of two kinds: **steps** and **half-steps**.

NOTE —These are sometimes erroneously called **tones** and **semi-tones**, but the objection to the use of the word **tone** for two purposes is obvious.

Statement 47. In harmony, where two or more tones are heard simultaneously, intervals are named, from their **harmonic effect**, **Seconds**, **Thirds**, **Fourths**, **Fifths**, **Sixths**,

THE ELEMENTS OF MUSIC.

Sevenths, and Eighths, or Octaves. The following diagram will show the order and kinds of harmonic intervals in the scale:

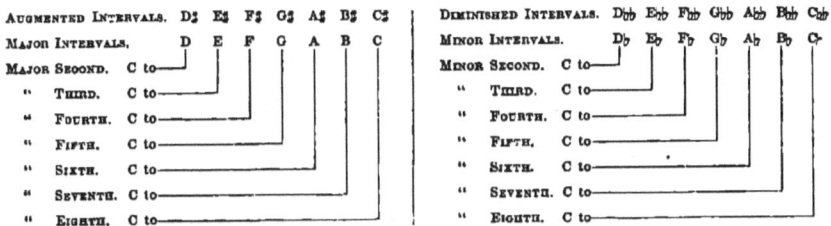

Statement 48. Of the seven intervals in the scale, five are **steps** and two are **half-steps**.

Statement 49. When the order of intervals in a scale is, from **one** to **two** a step, **two** to **three** a step, **three to four** a half-step, **four to five**, **five to six**, **six** to **seven**, each a step, and from **seven** to **eight** a half-step, such a scale is called the **Diatonic major** scale.

When the order of intervals is, **step, half-step, step, step, half-step, step,** and **step,** it is called the **Natural minor** scale.

When the order is, **step, half-step, step, step, half-step, step** and a **half,** and **half step,** it is called the **Harmonic minor** scale.

When the order is, **step, half-step, step, step, step, step,** and **half-step,** it is called the **Melodic minor** scale.

Statement 50. Between those tones of the scale where there is the interval of a **step,** there is an intermediate tone, named both from the tone next **below** and also the tone next **above** it.

When named from the tone **below,** the word **sharp,** meaning **higher,** is prefixed, as **sharp-one,** etc., and when named from the tone **above,** the word **flat,** meaning **lower,** is prefixed, as **flat-two,** etc.

Statement 51. The tones of the Diatonic scale and the five intermediate tones included, taken together, form the Chromatic scale, the intervals of which are all half-steps, as,

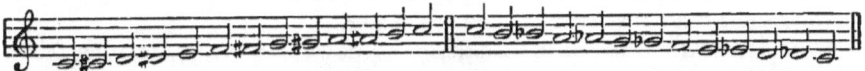

Statement 52. Those tones which constitute the Diatonic scale are called constituent or Diatonic tones, and those which are intermediate are called **Chromatic** tones. A Chromatic tone of **one** key may be a Diatonic tone of **another,** as, **sharp-four** in the key of C is **seven** in the key of G.

Statement 53. In applying absolute pitch-names to tones, C is first taken as **one** of a scale.

This being the case, since absolute pitch is unchangeable, the intervals between C and D, D and E, F and G, G and A, A and B are **always** steps, or major seconds, and between E and F, and B and C are **always** half-steps, or minor seconds.

Statement 54. Since the pitch of the scale may be changed, and any absolute pitch be taken as **one,** such change of pitch is called **transposition of the scale.**

Statement 55. The terms scale and key are often used synonymously. A scale or key is named from the pitch-name of **one,** which is called the **key-note,** or **key-tone.**

THE ELEMENTS OF MUSIC.

Statement 56. In transposing the scale, the order of intervals is preserved by the use of such chromatic or other tones as are needed, and the disuse of such as are not needed.

Statement 57. In first transposing the scale, the pitch G is taken as **one**, in the formation of which scale, F-sharp is taken instead of F, to preserve the right order of intervals.

Statement 58. The pitches constituting the scale of G are named G, A, B, C, D, E, F♯, and G.

Statement 59. The signature or sign of a key is placed after the clef, and the signature of the key of G is one sharp.

Statement 60. The pitch G is **five** of the scale of C, and, when taken as **one**, the scale is said to be transposed a **fifth**.

Statement 61. Every signature indicates two keys—a **major** key and its **relative minor**.

Statement 62. The relative minor of any major key begins with the tone **six** of that key, as, the relative minor of the key of C major is A minor, and of G Major is E Minor, etc.

Statement 63. In the **second** transposition by fifths, D is taken as **one**, the pitches named D, E, F♯, G, A, B, C♯, and D, being needed to preserve the right order of intervals.

Statement 64. The signature of the key of D is two sharps.

Statement 65. The relative minor of D major is B minor.

Statement 66. In the **third** transposition A is **one**, and the pitches A, B, C♯, D, E, F♯, G♯, and A constitute the scale.

Statement 67. The signature of the key of A is three sharps.

Statement 68. The relative minor of A major is F♯.

Statement 69. In the **fourth** transposition E is **one**, and the pitches E, F♯, G♯, A, B, C♯, D♯, and E constitute the scale.

Statement 70. The signature of the key of E is four sharps.

Statement 71. The relative minor of E major is C♯ minor.

Statement 72. In the **fifth** transposition B becomes **one**, and B, C♯, D♯, E, F♯, G♯, A♯, and B form the scale.

Statement 73. The signature of the key of B is five sharps.

Statement 74. The relative minor of B major is G♯.

Statement 75. In the **sixth** transposition by fifths the pitches F♯, G♯, A♯, B, C♯, D♯, E♯, and F♯ constitute the scale.

Statement 76. The signature of the key of F♯ is six sharps.

Statement 77. The relative minor of F♯ major is D♯.

Statement 78. The scale may be transposed by **fourths** as well as by **fifths**, in which case F first becomes **one**. In the formation of the scale of F, the pitch B♭ is needed, instead of B, to preserve the right order of intervals.

Statement 79. The pitches constituting the scale of F, are F, G, A, B♭, C, D, E, and F.

Statement 80. The signature of the key of F is one flat.

Statement 81. The relative minor of the key of F major is D.

Statement 82. In the second transposition by fourths, B♭ becomes one, and the pitches named B♭, C, D, E♭, F, G, A, and B♭ constitute the scale.

Statement 83. The signature of the key of B♭ is two flats.

Statement 84. The relative minor of B♭ major is G.

THE ELEMENTS OF MUSIC.

Statement 85. In the third transposition by fourths, E♮ becomes one, and the pitches constituting the scale are named E♭, F, G, A♭, B♭, C, D, and E♭.

Statement 86. The signature of the key of E♭ is three flats.

Statement 87. The relative minor of E♭ major is C.

Statement 88. In the fourth transposition by fourths, the pitches named A♭, B♭, C, D♭, E♭, F, G, and A♮ constitute the scale.

Statement 89. The signature of the key of A♭ is four flats.

Statement 90. The relative minor of A♭ major is F.

Statement 91. In the fifth transposition by fourths, the pitches D♭, E♭, F, G♭, A♭, B, C, and D♮ constitute the scale.

Statement 92. The signature of the key of D♭ is five flats.

Statement 93. The relative minor of D♭ major is B♭.

Statement 94. In the sixth transposition by fourths, the pitches G♭, A♭, B♭, C♭, D♭, E♭, F, and G♮ constitute the scale.

Statement 95. The signature of the key of G♭ is six flats.

Statement 96. The relative minor of G♭ major is E♭.

Statement 97. There are **twelve** scales differing in pitch, though only **seven** scale positions, as follows:

NOTE.—It will be seen by the above diagram that the number of flats or sharps in the two signatures, which make a given degree of the staff represent **one**, when added together, make the number **seven**. Therefore, if the number of **sharps** which make a given degree represent **one**, be taken from **seven**, the difference will be the number of **flats** required to make the same degree represent **one**, and *vice versa*.

Statement 98. In the diagram on page 10 the pitches constituting the chromatic scale, together with each major scale, and its relative harmonic minor, are indicated, and also the signature of each.

Statement 99. Changing the **name** of a tone without changing its pitch is called an **Enharmonic** change, as, C♯ becomes D♭; or, flat-two becomes sharp-one, etc.

NOTE.—To render a piece of music properly, three things are absolutely indispensable, namely: 1st. A perfect knowledge of its notation; 2d. The ability to perform it as written; and 3d. *The proper conception of the music.* The first two are the skeleton, and the last is the flesh and blood, the life.

A proper idea of those fine degrees of light and shade, of force, quality, and movement necessary to the latter can be but imperfectly conveyed by musical notation.

Some of the terms, abbreviations, and characters used for this purpose, are given in the statements which follow.

10   THE ELEMENTS OF MUSIC.

THE ELEMENTS OF MUSIC.

Statement 100. Different degrees of **force** and **quality** are indicated by certain words, abbreviations, or signs, of which there are many. The more common are as follows:

Pianissimo, (pp). Very soft.
Piano, (p). Soft.
Mezzo, (m). Medium.
Forte, (f). Loud.
Fortissimo, (ff). Very loud.
mf and *mp* are sometimes used, and also *ppp* and *pppp*.
Crescendo, or *cres.,* or ◁═. Gradually increasing.
Diminuendo, or *dim.,* } or ═▷. Gradually diminishing.
Decrescendo, or *decres.,* }
Swell, ◁══▷. Increase and diminish.
Forzando, (fz.) } or ▷. Suddenly diminishing from loud to soft.
Sforzando, (sfz). }
Affetuoso. With tenderness.
Agitato. Agitated.
Cantabile. In a graceful, singing style.

Calando,
Morendo,
Perdendosi, } Gradually fading away.
Smorzando,
Diluendo.
Dolce. Sweetly.
Con Energico. With energy.
Con Dolore. Sorrowfully.
Maestoso. Majestic.
Leggiero. Lightly and gaily.
Risoluto. With resolution.
Grazioso. Gracefully.
Con Espressione. With expression.
Con Fuoco. With fire.
Legato. Smooth and connected.
Con Spirito. With spirit.
Vigoroso. With vigor.

Statement 101. Different degrees of movement are indicated by certain words written over the music at the beginning; or, wherever any change of movement is desired.

These movement-words are many, and there is some conflict of authority with regard to the meaning of some of them. They may be divided into five general classes as indicated below, and they are arranged in that order of movement, from **slow** to **fast**, which accords most nearly with the best authorities. The author has never seen a list of these words given from which any other than a **general** idea of movement could be obtained. He undertakes here, as far as able, to give about the metronome movement indicated by each word, and if he errs, and shall bring upon himself criticism, and cause discussion to such an extent as to bring about some method of indicating movement more definitely in these terms, to have been the object of such censure will have been amply compensated for.

The figures placed in the column before each word indicate the number of beats in a minute. See next statement.

Slowest Movement.		Slow.		Medium.		Fast.		Fastest.	
40	Grave.	80	Lento.	110	Moderato.	145	Allegro.	175	Allegro Vivace.
50	Largo.	90	Andante.	120	Allegretto.	155	Animato.	185	Allegro Assai.
60	Larghetto.	100	Andantino.	130	Allegro Moderato.	165	Allegro Agitato.	195	Presto.
70	Adagio.							210	Prestissimo.

Statement 102. The movement of a piece is sometimes indicated by figures placed at the beginning of the piece, and, wherever in the piece a change of time is desired, thus, ♩ = 60, meaning that a tone represented by a **half-note** should be sung **one second long**, or 60 in a minute. Again, ♩ = 80, meaning that one-eightieth of a minute in time should be given to each tone represented by a quarter note, etc. An instrument called a **Metronome**, said to have been invented by Mælzel in 1815, and moved by clock-work, is employed to measure tone-lengths accurately. It consists of a graduated pendulum, marked somewhat after the manner of a thermometer, on which is a sliding weight which regulates the movement. This weight, placed at 80, would cause the pendulum to vibrate 80 times in a minute, or moved to any number would cause it to vibrate as many times in a minute as the number indicates.

THE ELEMENTS OF MUSIC.

A simpler method, proposed by Gottfried Weber, is a piece of twine, 55 inches in length, with a bullet or other weight attached and marked off into inch spaces. This set in motion vibrates 50 times in a minute; shortened to 50 inches, vibrates 52 times in a minute; 47 inches vibrates 54 times; 44 inches, 56; 41 inches, 58; 38 inches, 60; 34 inches, 63; 14 inches, 100 times, and to 5 inches 160 times.

Statement 103. The regular movement of a piece of music is temporarily interrupted or modified at times. Such interruptions are indicated by certain words, or their abbreviations, as follows:

Ritardando, Ritard, or *Rit.*
Ritenuto, Rit. } Gradually slower.
Rallentando, Rallen. Lentando.
Tempo rubato. Robbed, or stolen time, for expression.
Accelerando, Accel. Gradually faster.
Piu mosso. Rather faster.
Stringendo. Hastening the time.
Ad libitum. Slow or fast, at pleasure.

The meaning of the above words and also of regular movement words may be modified by the use of the following words:

Meno. Less.
Molto. Much.
Non troppo. Not too much.

Piu. More.
Un poco. A little.
Poco a poco. Little by little.

When the regular movement is again desired, after an interruption of it, it is indicated by the following:

A tempo. In time.
Tempo primo. First or original time.
Tempo giusto. In exact time.

Statement 104. As the whole compass of tones distinguishable to the human ear consists of about 9 scales or octaves, it seems desirable to have some means of designating the different pitches. The manner of doing this is indicated in the diagram on next page, and, as will be seen, is by the use of small and capital letters, marked and unmarked.

Statement 105. The range or the compass of the ordinary human voice is about two octaves, though some have less and some greater compass. Voices are generally divided into four classes and named from lower to higher: Bass, Tenor, Alto and Soprano. The following diagram indicates their average compass:

Some Base singers sing as low as C or B, some Tenors as high as c, some Altos as low as d, and some Sopranos as high as f or g. See diagram on next page.

THE ELEMENTS OF MUSIC.

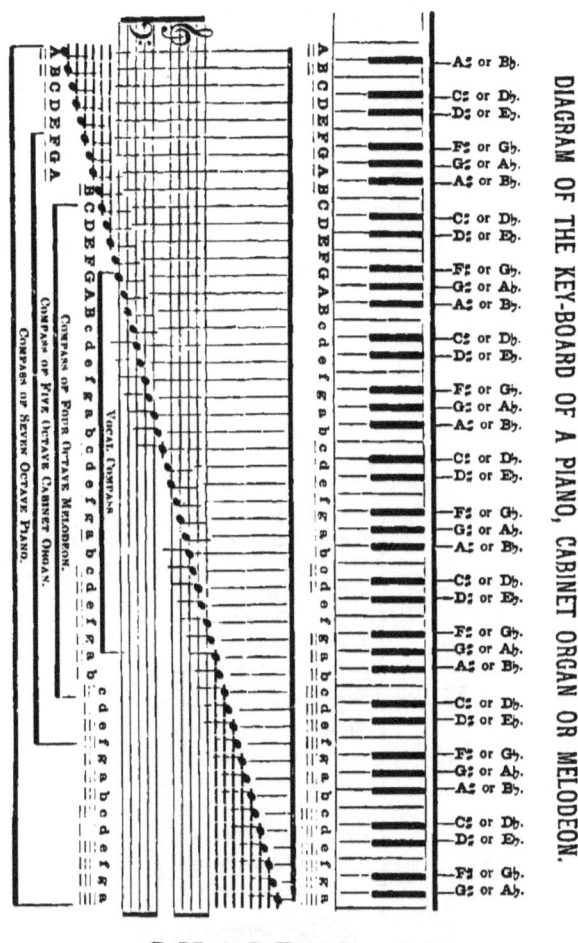

CHAPTER II.

THE following diagrams, it is believed, will prove of service to those who have not time to give the subjects more extended examination.

First, the names of the different kinds of voices and instruments and their ordinary compass are given.

Second, is a classification of collections of voices and instruments.

Third, a list of the numbers and kinds of instruments used in orchestras or bands of from ten to one hundred performers, though different teachers might make some slight modification of the number of certain instruments according to their fancy.

Fourth, the majority of instruments mentioned are represented in a page taken, by permission, from WEBSTER'S NATIONAL PICTORIAL DICTIONARY.

Fifth, is given the names and brief description of the different classes of musical composition, sacred and secular, in use.

THE ELEMENTS OF MUSIC.

NAMES OF DIFFERENT KINDS OF VOICES AND INSTRUMENTS, AND THEIR COMPASS.

VOICES.
- Soprano. The highest female voice. Compass, c to c, and sometimes f.
- Mezzo-Soprano. The most common female voice. Compass, b to g.
- Contralto. / Alto. } The lowest female voice. Compass, e or f to d or e.
- Tenor. The highest male voice. Compass, c to c.
- Baritone. The most common male voice. Compass, G to f and g.
- Base. The lowest male voice. Compass C or D to d.

INSTRUMENTS.

STRINGED.
- Banjo. An instrument with six strings. Compass, g to c.
- Base-Viol. / Violoncello. } An instrument with four strings. Compass, E to a.
- Double-Base. Having four strings. Compass, E to g.
- Dulcimer. A triangular instrument having about fifty wire strings.
- Guitar. / Cittern. } Having six strings. Compass, e to c.
- Harp. Having many strings. Compass, C to f.
- Clavecin. / Clavichord. / Harpsichord. } A rude piano of olden time.
- Lute. / Cithara. } Having six strings. Compass from g to c.
- Lyre. Having eight strings.
- Piano. Compass from A to c.
- Viola. Having four strings. Compass from c to f.
- Viol da gamba. Having six strings.
- Violin. Having four strings. Compass from g to c.

WIND.

Brass.
- Bugle. Compass from b to c.
- Cornet. Compass from g to c. Different sizes.
- French Horn. Compass from C to c.
- Ophicleide. / Tuba. } Compass, B to c. Different sizes.
- Sax-Horn. Compass, g to c.
- Trombone. Compass from E♭ to f.
- Trumpet. Compass from C to a.

Wood.
- Bassoon. / Fagotto. } Compass from B♭ to b♭.
- Clarinet. Compass from e to g.
- Cor Anglais. Compass from e to b♭.
- Fife. Compass from d to d.
- Flageolet. Compass from c to c.
- Flute. Compass from c to a.
- Hautboy. / Oboe. } Compass from b to f.
- Piccolo. Compass from f to c.

With Bellows.
- Accordion. / Concertina. } Compass from g to g.
- Bagpipe. A favorite instrument with the Scotch.
- Cabinet Organ. / Harmonium. / Melodeon. } For compass, see page 13.
- Organ. Compass varying from seven to nine octaves.

PERCUSSION.
- Castanets.
- Cymbals.
- Base Drum.
- Kettle Drum.
- Snare or Side Drum.
- Tabor.
- Tamborine.
- Timbrel.
- Triangle.

Among these instruments, the Kettle Drum is tuned to definite pitch, two being used in orchestras and tuned to *fifths* or *fourths* of the keys in which they play.

THE ELEMENTS OF MUSIC. 15

CLASSIFICATION OF COLLECTIONS OF VOICES AND INSTRUMENTS.

- **Solo.** Music in **one** part, for **one** voice or instrument.
- **Duet.** Music in **two** parts, for **two** voices or instruments.
- **Trio.** Music in **three** parts, for **three** voices or instruments.
- **Quartette.** Music in **four** parts, for **four** voices or instruments.
- **Quintette.** Music in **five** parts, for **five** voices or instruments.
- **Sextet.** Music in **six** parts, for **six** voices or instruments.
- **Septet.** Music in **seven** parts, for **seven** voices or instruments.
- **Octet.** Music in **eight** parts, for **eight** voices or instruments.
- **Choir.** A collection of singers of indefinite number, organized for stated and regular service.
- **Chorus.** A term applied more properly to a large collection of singers.
- **Semi-Chorus.** A collection of singers, less in number than the chorus.
- **Soli.** Each part with a single or solo voice. The plural of Solo.
- **Tutti.** All of the voices—used in a piece where a part is Soli.

ORCHESTRA.
1. The place in a theatre or concert-room occupied by the band.
2. The collection of players on instruments of varied quality and compass.

BANDS.
- **Brass Band.** A collection of players on **brass** wind-instruments.
- **String Band.** A band consisting only of **stringed** instruments played with a bow.
- **Wind Band.** } **Wood Band.** } The players on **wood** wind-instruments, as, clarionet, flute, &c.
- **Military Band.** A band connected with military service using brass instruments chiefly, with clarionets and flutes at times.

ORCHESTRA.

Number of Performers.	10	15	20	30	40	50	75	100
1st Violin.	2	2	3	6	8	10	16	20
2d Violin.	1	2	2	4	6	6	10	16
Viola.	1	1	1	2	4	4	8	14
Violoncello.	..	1	1	2	3	4	8	12
Double Bass.	1	1	1	2	3	4	8	12
Flute.	1	1	1	1	1	2	2	2
Clarionet.	2	2	2	2	2	2	2	2
Cornet.	1	1	2	2	2	2	2	2
Trombone.	1	1	1	1	1	3	3	3
French Horn.	..	2	2	2	4	4	4	4
Hautboy.	..	..	1	2	2	2	2	2
Kettle Drum.	..	1	1	1	1	1	1	1
Bassoon.	..	..	1	2	2	2	2	2
Piccolo.	..	..	1	1	1	1	1	1
Snare Drum	..	..	..	..	..	1	1	1
Bass Drum.	..	..	..	..	..	.	1	1
Tuba.	..	..	..	..	..	1	1	1
Harp.	..	..	..	..	..	1	1	1
Bass Clarinet.	..	..	..	..	..	..	1	1
Cor Anglais.	..	..	..	..	..	..	1	1
Cymbals.	..	..	..	..	..	..	..	1
Triangle.	..	..	..	..	..	..	..	1
Tambourine.	..	..	..	..	..	..	..	1

BRASS BAND.

Number of Performers.	10	15	20	30	40
E♭ Cornet.	2	3	3	3	3
B♭ Cornet.	2	3	3	6	8
E♭ Alto Cornet.	2	3	3	4	5
B♭ Tenor Cornet.	2	2	2	3	4
B♭ Baritone Tuba.	1	1	1	2	2
E♭ Tuba.	1	2	2	3	4
B♭ Bass.	..	1	1	1	2
E♭ Piccolo.	..	..	1	1	1
E♭ Clarionet.	..	..	1	2	3
B♭ Clarionet.	..	..	3	5	6

MUSICAL INSTRUMENTS.

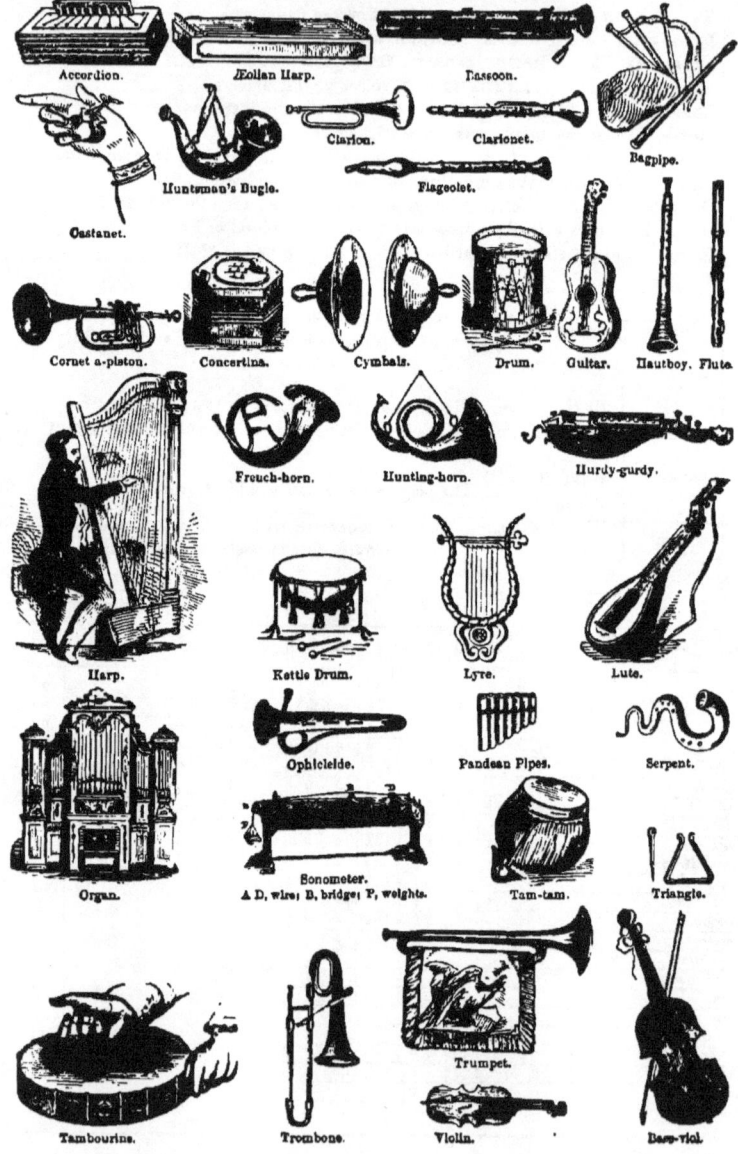

THE ELEMENTS OF MUSIC. 17

NAMES OF DIFFERENT FORMS OF MUSICAL COMPOSITION.

VOCAL.

SACRED.

Anthem. A composition in chorus and solo parts, set to scriptural words, and of moderate length.
Cantata. A short work in the form of an oratorio, with solos, duets, etc.
Carol. A song of praise, usually applied to a kind of songs sung at Christmas-time.
Chant. A short composition to which the Psalms or verses of irregular length are sung or recited.
Choral. A hymn or Psalm-tune of slow movement, used largely in Germany.
Dirge. A piece of solemn character, used chiefly on funereal occasions.
Doxology. A hymn or song of praise, used often at the close of religious services.
Introit. In modern use, a short anthem used at the beginning of religious services.
Mass. Portions of the Catholic service set to music, often of a varied and difficult character.
Motet. Differing little, in modern use, from the introit or anthem.
Oratorio. A composition, the most extended of sacred forms. It was designed for voices and instruments, and intended to illustrate some scripture subject, unchanged or paraphrased.
Recitative. A form of composition in which words are musically recited or declaimed. Used in Oratorio and Opera chiefly.
Requiem. A composition of considerable length, sung in honor of distinguished dead.
Vespers. The evening song in the Roman Catholic church.

SECULAR.

Aria. A song of various forms, often of difficult execution and capable of much musical expression.
Ballad. A brief story told in simple verse, and set to a short, familiar air.
Barcarole. A simple boat song, imitating the songs of the Venetian gondolier.
Canon. A kind of perpetual fugue, in which the parts repeat the same tune or melody one after another, often at different pitch.
Catch. A kind of canon in three or four parts, the words being so arranged that a different meaning is given by *catching* at them.
Cavatina. A song simpler in form than the aria.
Glee. A composition in three or four parts, consisting of two or more contrasted movements, or interwoven melodies.
Madrigal. A composition of considerable difficulty, often in five or six parts.
Opera. In *secular* music what the oratorio is in *sacred*. A secular drama. It consists of solos, recitatives, duets, trios, choruses, etc.
Operetta. In *secular* music what the cantata is in *sacred*. A short opera.
Serenade. A composition of a quiet, soothing character, for use at night in the open air.

INSTRUMENTAL.

Chaconne. A slow dance in $\frac{3}{4}$ time.
Concerto. A composition to display the qualities of some particular instrument; as violin, violoncello, piano, etc. A short symphony.
Fantasia. A fancy of the composer, with little regard to form.
Fugue. Similar to the canon, though more elaborate.
Galop. A lively dance in $\frac{2}{4}$ time.
Gavotte. A dance, lively, yet dignified, and a favorite movement in sonatas in the 17th century.
Hornpipe. An English dance, named from the instrument on which it was played.
Impromptu. A piece played without previous thought or preparation.
Interlude. A piece either prepared or impromptu, played between the stanzas of a hymn, or acts of a drama.
Jig. A lively dance-tune in triple time, which may be danced by one or more dancers.
Mazurka. A Polish grotesque dance, the music being in $\frac{3}{8}$ or $\frac{3}{4}$ time.
Nocturne. A kind of instrumental serenade.
Overture. An instrumental piece, introductory to some special work; as, opera, etc.
Polka. A very popular dance, the music for which is in $\frac{2}{4}$ time.
Prelude. An introduction to a musical work, or performance.
Quadrille. A favorite dance, the music being in four movements.
Rondo. A composition in three movements, after the symphonic form.
Schottische. A slow Scotch dance of modern introduction, in $\frac{3}{4}$ time.
Sonata. A composition of the highest order for a single instrument, in three and sometimes four movements.
Symphony. A composition for orchestra, of similar construction to the sonata, consisting generally of allegro, andante, scherzo or playful, and allegro movements.
Waltz. Valse. A Bohemian dance in triple time. Compositions of a higher order take the same movement, but are not intended for the dance.
Voluntary. An organ solo played at any time during church service, and may be impromptu or selected.

CHAPTER III.

A BRIEF TREATISE ON HARMONY.

It is believed that a brief explanation of the use of the chords most frequently used in musical compositions might be profitably introduced here. By **Melody** is meant a succession of tones, produced by a single voice, arranged usually after some rhythmic plan, to produce a pleasing effect. By **Harmony** is meant the addition of one or more tones to each tone of a melody, and sung simultaneously with it, and so combined as also to produce a pleasing effect. **Three tones**, heard simultaneously, arranged in the order of **one, three** and **five** to each other, are called a **Triad**, or **Common Chord**. The tone on which the triad is formed, and from which it is named, is called its **Root**, or **Fundamental Tone**.

Triads are of three kinds, **Major, Minor,** and **Diminished.**

A **Major** triad consists of a tone and its major third and a major or perfect fifth. See *Statement* 47.

A **Minor** triad consists of a tone and its minor third and major fifth.

A **Diminished** triad consists of a tone and its minor third and minor fifth.

In writing music in four parts, or for four different voices, we repeat or double one of the tones of the triad, usually the **octave** to the **root**, though one of the others may be doubled.

The term **Common Chord**, with us, usually is used for **Triad.**

These chords are indicated and named in the scale below:

| C Major. | D Minor. | E Minor. | F Major. | G Major. | A Minor. | B Diminished. | C Major. |
| Tonic. | Supertonic. | Mediant. | Subdominant. | Dominant. | Superdominant. | Subtonic. | Tonic. |

Of course the same order occurs relatively in every major scale.

A major chord may be changed to a minor chord by changing its third, and to a diminished chord by changing its third and fifth, as above, in first measure.

The tones of the scale are distinguished in harmony by the names given above, under the names of the triads or chords.

It will be seen by referring to the above diagram that there are **three major** chords in the scale, the **Tonic, Subdominant,** and **Dominant** chords, and since these are used more frequently in harmony than any others, their use will be briefly explained here. These three chords contain all of the tones of the scale as the following diagram shows; and also that while the Subdominant and Dominant chords have each one tone belonging to the Tonic, they have none belonging to each other. This fact will be more painfully apparent as we proceed.

Observe also that each chord may have three **positions**; as, when **one** or **eight** is **highest,** it is in the **first** position; when **three is highest,** the **second** position; and when **five** is highest, the **third** position.

```
c — e — g — — c
1   3   5     8
    f — a — c
    4   6   8
        g — b — d
        5   7   2
```

Ex. 2.   1st Position.   2d Position.   3d Position.

When the tones of a chord are represented **close** to each other, as at 1 above, it is called **close** harmony; and when **scattered**, as at 2, it is called **dispersed** harmony.

Let us now begin to make practical use of that about which we have been speaking, and in a familiar way, as between teacher and pupil. Let us take a line of some stanza and harmonize it, using one chord, being careful to keep **near shore**, or where we can understand what we are doing.

Take this line: "The soft winds creep along the sea;" and let us begin.

Ex. 3.

The soft winds creep a - long the sea.

Sing it, and state objections, if any. **Objection 1st.** The **accent** of the **music** does not agree with the **accent** of the **words**. The first word or syllable, being **unaccented**, should begin or end with an **unaccented** part of the measure, and therefore should begin with the **second** part of the measure; or, it might have a **long** tone, so that the **accented** syllable "soft" could begin with the first or accented part of the second measure. Now that the attention is directed to it, remember that the accent of words and music must correspond.

Objection 2d. Each part continues with the tone with which it begins, and is therefore monotonous, or does not **move**, or has no **motion**. To avoid this monotony, while we can use but **one chord**, we remember that a chord may be used in **different positions**, which will afford some relief.

Objection 3d. The harmony is too **close**, and needs **scattering** or **dispersing**.

Objection 4th. The Alto is written on the Base staff.

Noting carefully these **objections** and the **remedy**, let us try again. Compare the above exercises marked (2) and (3), and observe if the accent in (4) agrees with the accents of the words. From the last we may learn that we may have some latitude in selecting the kind of measure to use, when we wish to write music to poetry.

While all of the parts in (2), (3), and (4) have motion but the **Base**, let us see if we can relieve the monotony of that part.

In Ex. 2 we have the Subdominant and Dominant chords mentioned as often used with the Tonic chord. Let us take the Dominant chord and use it with the Tonic, remembering the injunction to keep **near shore**. The pitches which compose the Dominant chord are **five**, **seven**, and **two** of any scale, or G, B, and D of the scale of C.

In the study of Harmony, **the movement or progression of the tones of one chord to those of another must be carefully observed.**

There are three forms of motion or progression—**Parallel, Contrary,** and **Oblique**.

Parallel motion is where two or more parts progress in the **same** direction, ascending or descending, and equidistant from each other.

Contrary motion is where the parts proceed in **opposite** directions.

Oblique motion is where one part remains **stationary**, while others move either in **parallel** or **contrary** motion.

Contrary motion is most effective, **Oblique** next, and **Parallel** the weakest. These three forms are illustrated below.

With what has been said above, let us now proceed.

The soft winds sweep along the sea.

After singing it, objection is made to the sound of the Base and Soprano, where they move from the Tonic to the Dominant chord and back again. By observation we discover that they move in **parallel** motion, and that the interval between the Base and Soprano at **a** is a **fifth**, and also at **b**, making thus what are called **consecutive** fifths, which are always to be avoided. The same occur at c and d, d and e, and e and f, between Base and Soprano. Before attempting to try again, perhaps we had better take the two chords and have several examples of using them in different positions, to make pleasant progressions in all parts.

Since the **fifth** in the **Tonic** chord is the **root** in the **Dominant** chord, and is the only tone belonging to both chords, it would be well for us in our first efforts to retain it in the **same** part, in moving from one chord to the other. Observe above, at (2), that the three positions of C are taken, and the progressions indicated; study them carefully.

Observe also the progressions at *j*, *k*, and *l*, where the tone common to both chords is not retained in the same part.

Let us now take a full stanza and see what we can do.

For fear we may confine our thoughts too closely to the key of C, let us use these chords in an exercise in the key of G. The Tonic chord in the key of G consists of G, B, and D, or what was Dominant in the key of C; and the Dominant chord in the key of G consists of D, F♯, and A. Of course, the same principles apply in the progression of chords in one key that apply in another, unless that, in some keys, some parts might move either **up** or **down**, to avoid being too **low** or **high**, which might in other keys move otherwise.

In the last chord above, the **fifth** is omitted, to avoid an awkward **melodic** progression in the Alto, though the **harmonic** progression would be correct to use D in the Alto. The **fifth** of a chord is sometimes omitted.

As our space will not allow an extended course in Harmony, and cannot therefore have many exercises illustrating the same point, we will next prepare an exercise using the Tonic and Subdominant chords.

In choosing between the combination of the Tonic and Dominant, and Tonic and Subdominant, the former would probably be chosen as most satisfactory. The union of the three in one combination will be more satisfactory, and to that we will now proceed.

We have already learned somewhat of the progression of the Tonic to the Dominant and back, and the same of the Tonic and Subdominant, each of these chords having one tone in common with the Tonic, and thus affording a bond of union. The Subdominant and Dominant have no tone in common; and where there is so much unlikeness, there is often a lack of harmony, and need of greater caution in progressing. Let us see the danger.

In the progression from the Subdominant to the Dominant chords above, it will be observed that between the Alto and Soprano, or Base and Soprano, there are, what have already been spoken of as unpleasant and objectionable, **consecutive fifths**, and also between Base and Alto, **consecutive octaves**. The objection to consecutive octaves is not that they **sound unpleasantly**, since in music we frequently have **unison passages**, in which case there must be consecutive octaves between Soprano and Base, but because thereby the parts are reduced to **three** in sound, instead of **four**, and the harmony is weakened. Let us improve this progression at (2), (3), and (4) above, using the different positions of each chord. Now let us apply the three chords in a song.

Ex. 10.

Sing a merry song together! Make the music full and strong! Hearts can ne'er be far asunder, When the voices join in song.

From the foregoing exercises it will be seen that it is quite possible to compose music consisting entirely of chords in their **direct** form, by which is meant, **having the root or fundamental tone of the chord in the Base.** Such progressions are often lacking in melody, especially in the Base, and, continued any great length of time, become wearisome and monotonous. Relief may be found by **inverting the chords,** by which is meant **taking or using some other tone in the Base than the root of the chord.**

As there are but **three** tones in the chord differing in pitch, so there can be but **two** inversions. When the Base has the **root** of the chord, the form is **direct.**

When the Base has the **third** of the chord, it is the **first** inversion.

When the Base has the **fifth** of the chord, it is the **second** inversion.

It is hoped the pupil will keep clearly in mind the distinction between the **position of the** chord, heretofore explained, and **inversion** of the chord, now explained and illustrated below.

Ex. 11.

Tonic.			Subdominant.			Dominant.		
Direct Form.	1st Inversion.	2d Inv.	Direct.	1st Inv.	2d Inv.	Direct.	1st Inv.	2d Inv.
3d Position.	1st Pos.	2d Pos.	2d Pos.	3d Pos.	1st Pos.	1st Pos.	3d Pos.	2d Pos.

At *a, b,* and *c* above, we have the direct form and the two inversions of the Tonic chord; at *d, e,* and *f* the same forms of the Subdominant; and at *g, h,* and *i* the same forms of the Dominant chord. Observe that in each inversion there are no tones but what belong to the direct form of the chord.

So long as the chord was **direct,** it was easy to tell what it was by looking at the Base. Now it is more difficult, and makes it necessary to analyze the chord in order to determine. Formerly, the inversions of the chord were indicated by certain figures placed **under the Base**, so that by looking at the Base and the figure, the form of the chord could be determined from or **through the Base**, from which, using the old English word **thorough** for **through**, we have the term **thorough Base**. The figure 6 is used for the **first** inversion, and the figures ⁶⁄₄ for the **second** inversion. Space will not allow further explanation of their use.

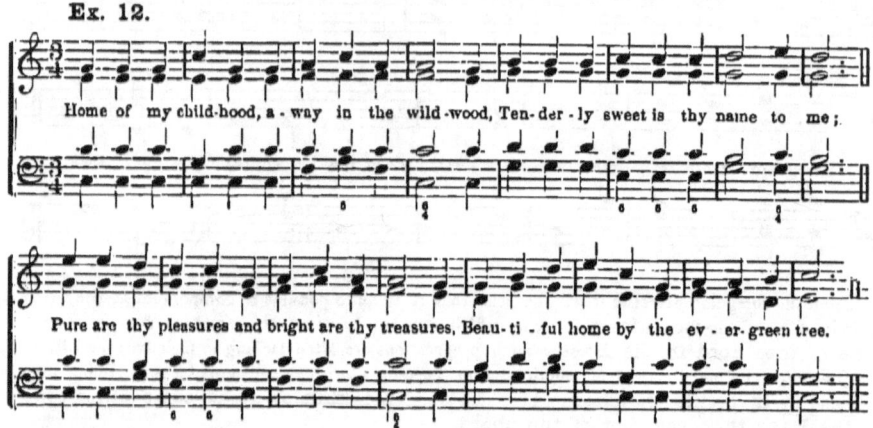

In using the Dominant chord, sometimes, instead of doubling the **root** of the chord, as, g, b, d, and g, the pitch f is taken, making the chord consist of g, b, d, and f. The relation of f to g being that of **seven** to one, this chord is called the chord of the **Dominant seventh**. It is frequently used, either direct or inverted, and is, in perhaps a majority of cases, the next to the last chord in a piece of music. Since the chord consists of four different tones, it will admit of three inversions, which, with the method of figuring each, are illustrated below, with the **Resolution**, which means, the chord to which this leads.

The most **common** resolution of this chord is into the **Tonic** chord. The **third** of this chord should not be omitted, and the **seventh** should **resolve** or **move** to the next tone below. Use the song on the next page as a Morning song, but analyze it and observe the use of the chords.

MORNING HYMN.

1. Give to our God immortal praise; Mercy and truth are all His ways;
2. Give to the Lord of lords renown, The King of kings with glory crown:
3. He built the earth, He spread the sky, And fixed the starry lights on high:
4. Through this vain world He guides our feet, And leads us to His heavenly seat:

Wonders of grace to God belong; Repeat His mercies in your song.
His mercies ever shall endure, When lords and kings are known no more.
Wonders of grace to God belong; Repeat His mercies in your song.
His mercies ever shall endure, When this vain world shall be no more.

In the first and second lines the parts all sing the same tones, and therefore sing in **Unison**. Unison passages are not infrequent in music.

We have had under consideration, briefly, the three **major** chords in the scale, founded on **one, four,** and **five,** and named Tonic, Subdominant, and Dominant. There are **two** of the three **Minor** chords found in the scale which are quite frequently used, the one founded on **two,** or the Super-Tonic, and the one founded on **six,** or the Super-dominant, or, as it might be called, the relative minor chord. The latter is more frequently used than the former, and into it the Dominant seventh chord is frequently resolved.

The Super-tonic chord is often used as one of the closing chords of a musical phrase or section and usually **direct,** or in its **first** inversion.

Observe the use of each of these chords in the following exercise:

Ex. 14.

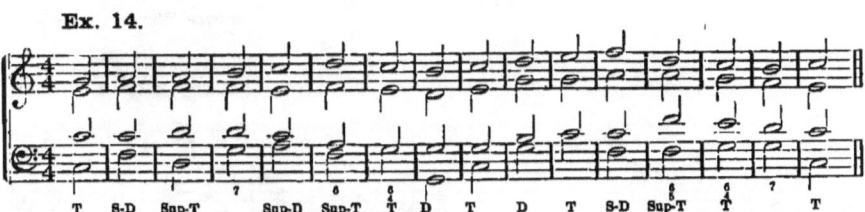

T S-D Sup-T Sup-D Sup-T T D T D T S-D Sup-T T T

The last two or three chords of a section or piece of music are called a **Cadence**. Cadences are of four kinds.

When the Tonic chord is preceded by the Dominant, it is called a **perfect,** or **Authentic** Cadence.

When the Tonic is preceded by the Subdominant chord, it is called a **Plagal** Cadence.

A BRIEF TREATISE ON HARMONY.

When the last chord is Dominant, preceded by the Tonic, it is called an **Imperfect**, or half Cadence.

When the Dominant chord is followed by some other chord than the Tonic, the Cadence is said to be **Interrupted**, false, or deceptive.

Ex. 15.

[musical example with labels: Perfect. Authentic. — Plagal. — Imperfect. — Interrupted, or Deceptive.]

The foregoing limited and brief treatise of the more prominent chords in use in music, it is hoped will be of service to those thoughtful persons or pupils who desire to know something about the subject in a general way, and do not hope to give sufficient attention to the subject to make practical use of it. From the chords given here, with their various positions and inversions, together with the many not given, with their various combinations and progressions, one will not be slow to understand how extensive is the field, and how inexhaustible the supply of melodic and harmonic forms which it contains.

Connected with this subject is that of **Modulation** and **Transition**, brief mention of which will here be made. By **Modulation** is meant the passing out of the key in which a piece of music begins, into another key nearly or closely related to it; as, from the key of C to G; or, C to F, D to A; or, E-flat to A-flat, &c. It is customary to return again to the original key. Sing the following beautiful song by Weber, and notice how it modulates into the key of C in the second line, and back to F in the last line.

If it is a little **hard** in one or two places, **work** and **master it.**

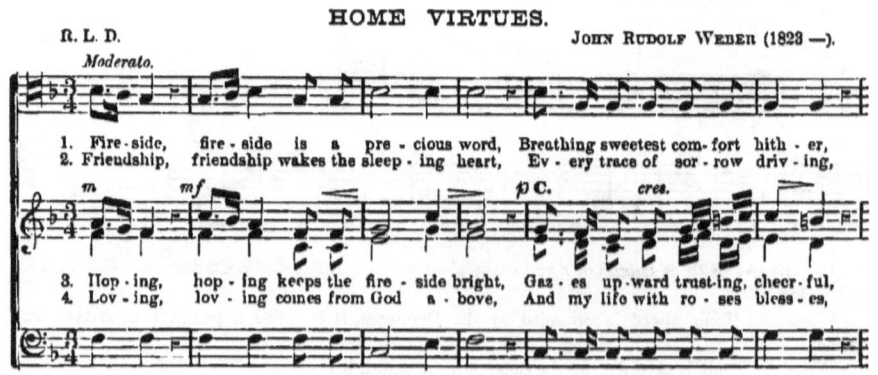

HOME VIRTUES.

R. L. D.   JOHN RUDOLF WEBER (1823 —).

A BRIEF TREATISE ON HARMONY.

The **majority** of modulations are from one key to that which is a **fifth higher**, or **fourth lower**, as from C to G, G to D, B♭ to F, and F to C, as in the above song. In the beautiful May Song, by Ecker, which follows, note the modulation from C to G, which is a **fifth higher**; then back to C, and then to F, which is a **fourth higher**, or **fifth lower**, which is perhaps the next modulation in the frequency of its use.

THE MAY IS HERE!

R. L. D., from FRED. OFER.
SOLI. *Spiritoso.*
CARL ECKER (1815 —).
TUTTI.

One more illustration of modulation will be given, in which it will be seen that there are **two** modulations by **fourths**, from D to G, and from G to C, and returning to the original key. Music of this character will require a little patience and perseverance to learn, but when well learned, it becomes "a thing of beauty," and, it might almost be added, "a joy forever."

The last one, by Braun, is to illustrate **Transition**, though it also illustrates **Modulation**.

By **Transition** is meant the passing abruptly, or suddenly, from one key to another key, remote from the one from which we pass.

In this song, the **modulation** is first into the key of G, and the **transition** from G into the key of E♭.

The pupil is referred to the body of the book for other illustrations, hoping that what has here been briefly and imperfectly said, will induce pupils to examine more carefully the structure of what they sing.

A BRIEF TREATISE ON HARMONY. 29

SIGNS OF SPRING.

CHAPTER IV.

BRIEF MUSICAL BIOGRAPHIES.

A BRIEF biographical sketch of several of the great composers is given here as a matter of interest to those who may not have the time or disposition for more extended reading. It is also hoped that because of some acquaintance with such of their works as are found in this work, a desire may be created to know more of their lives and their works. They will be mentioned in the order of their birth.

George Frederic Handel was born in Halle, in the duchy of Magdeburg in Lower Saxony, on the 24th of February, 1684 or 1685, there being some conflict of authority as to which year. He was the son of a surgeon, who desired him to study law. His passion for music predominated, and he was placed under the instruction of Zachau, an organist, and at nine years of age officiated at the organ, and began the study and practice of composition. In 1704 his first opera, "Almira," was performed; and the second, "Nero," in 1705. From 1708 to 1710 he visited Italy and Venice. He returned to Germany early in 1710, and late in that year went to London, where he spent the chief part of his life. He was a voluminous composer, composing a large number of operas, cantatas, sonatas, oratorios, etc.

His oratorio, the "Messiah," is his masterpiece, and is performed far and near by such musical societies as desire to study the highest order of music. He died April 13, 1759, and his remains are deposited among the noted ones in Westminster Abbey, London.

John Sebastian Bach was born at Eisenach, March 21, 1685. He was of a musical family, there being many of that name of some eminence as musicians and composers. He was especially eminent as an organist and composer of organ music. In *fugue* music he stands at the head, many of his fugues being so intricate as to be performed only by organists of superior ability. His vocal compositions partake somewhat of this order, and are not very much used. He died at Leipsic, July 30, 1750.

Francis Joseph Haydn (pronounced Hyden) was born at Rohrau, about 45 miles from Vienna, March 31, 1732. His father was a wheelwright and parish sexton. In humble circumstances, and often in penury and want, he struggled to obtain a knowledge of his chosen art, singing soprano in a parish choir until his voice broke at the late age of nineteen years. Before him, it is said, no one had an idea of an orchestra of eighteen different instruments, so that in the direction of music for orchestral instruments he established a new order of things. He composed 527 instrumental compositions.

In 1790 he visited London, and again in 1794, after which he returned to Austria to remain. In London he became acquainted and delighted with Handel's music, and in 1795 began his oratorio, the "Creation," on which he worked two years, and of which he said, "I am long about it, for 1 wish it to last long." Two years later he composed the oratorio, the "Four Seasons." The "Creation" ranks with the "Messiah" as a masterpiece. He died May 31, 1809, at Gumpendorff.

Johann Chrysostomus Wolfgang Gottlieb Mozart (Mo-tsart) was born at Salzburg, January 27, 1756. His father was a musician and teacher, and gave lessons on the violin and harpsichord. When *three* years of age his delight was to find thirds on the harpsichord; at *four* he could play several minuets and other pieces on the harpsichord; at *five* he began to compose some trifling pieces. At six years the family removed to Munich, where he soon learned to play the violin. Of his remarkable musical talent, for which he was greatly admired and praised, he seemed neither forward nor vain. At *seven*, the family removed to Paris, and at *eight* to London, where he composed six sonatos.

At *ten*, he returned to Salzburg, where he studied composition, taking as models Handel, Bach, and Hasse. A sister, four years older than himself, was a fine performer on the harpsichord, and together they performed in public in the principal cities. At thirteen they went to Italy. At Rome he heard Allegri's Miserere in the Sistine chapel, which so impressed him as to lead him thereafter to adopt a more serious style in composition.

At fifteen, while in Italy, he composed his first opera, "Mithridate." He was married at twenty-six, and soon after went to Vienna, where he remained in the service of the emperor at the nominal salary of 800 florins. When asked what he received, he wrote, "Too much for what I have done; too little for what I might have done." Haydn and Mozart had each great respect for the ability of the other, but Mozart esteemed Handel most of all, and says of him, "He understands better than all of us how to produce a grand effect." His masterpieces are the operas, "Magic Flute," "Clemenza di Tito," "Don Giovanni," and his "Requiem," which was written for one who desired it to commemorate the death of a dear friend in a solemn yearly service, but it proved to be the funeral hymn of the great composer, who finished it a few days before his death, December 5, 1792.

Louis Van Beethoven (Bay-tó-ven) was born December 17, 1770, at Bonn, on the Rhine. His father was a tenor singer, and Louis a stubborn, impatient boy, who had to be driven to the piano, though loving music in his own way.

In his fifteenth year he was appointed organist to the Elector of Cologne. At twenty-two he went to Vienna to receive instruction from Haydn. He was never married. At thirty he had composed two symphonies, over twenty sonatos, trios, etc. He composed but one oratorio, "Mount of Olives," and one opera, "Fidelio."

His was a sensitive nature, and being afflicted with deafness, he secluded himself from society. In a letter to his brother, he says, "It is not possible for me to say to people, 'speak louder, bawl, for I am deaf.' Almost alone in the world, I dare not venture into society more than absolute necessity requires." His devotion to his art, in which he was often unconscious of what was passing, or even his own wants, led him into many peculiarities and eccentricities. On one occasion it is said that he went to an inn, and seating himself by the table became buried in thought. After some time, he arose and asked for his indebtedness, forgetting that he had ordered nothing.

In the latter years of his life his deafness became almost total, and with failure of health, anxiety about subsistence, intrigues of enemies, etc., he became greatly depressed. His greatest works are his nine Symphonies, which have never been superseded nor equalled. In the ninth and last symphony, having exhausted orchestral effects, it occurred to him to introduce a chorus of voices, in which he used Schiller's "Hymn to Joy." He says, "The secret of all true art lies, after all, in the *moral*." He died March 26, 1827, in Vienna, where he had spent the greater part of his life.

BRIEF MUSICAL BIOGRAPHIES.

Felix Mendelssohn Bartholdy was born in Hamburg, Feb. 3, 1808. He was the son of a rich merchant and banker, and his mother being of the Bartholdy family, out of regard to her, the name Bartholdy was added to his. He early became a convert to the Christian faith, and entered the Lutheran church in Berlin. The distinguished German author, Goethe, was among the first noted ones to interest himself in his remarkable genius. At six, he exhibited marked skill upon the piano; at eight, could play Bach's intricate fugues; and at nine, gave his first concert in Berlin, and at ten, his first in Paris. He then began composing for the piano, violin, viola, and violoncello, and several of the quartettes, written before he was fifteen, still rank among classical works.

His overture to "Midsummer Night's Dream" was composed in 1826, and now, as then, is greatly admired. His first opera was given in 1827, and was unsuccessful. In 1835 he went from Berlin to Leipsic, to direct the famous Gewandhaus concerts. His oratorio, "St. Paul," was first performed at Leipsic and Düsseldorf, and in 1837, under his own direction, at the Birmingham Festival in England. His oratorio, "Elijah," was written for this festival, where it was first performed, Aug. 26, 1846. He was nine years in composing it. His "Songs without Words," for the piano, are gems of beauty and expression, and are unequalled. His life was free from the trials and struggles of some of the masters who preceded him, and his beauty of character gained for him as much regard as his genius.

He died at Leipsic, November 2, 1847.

NOTE.—The six composers mentioned, unquestionably stand at the head of all musical composers, past or present. There are, however, several who have contributed largely of *songs for the people*, whose names are deserving of mention here.

Hans Georg Nageli was born in Zurich, in 1768, where in 1792 he began to publish a choice collection from the classical masters. He also composed many songs which became popular, among which his "Life let us cherish" is everywhere known. Of this Gerber says, "How happy must a composer feel, could he enjoy during his life even a thousandth part of the harmless pleasure imparted to his fellow-creatures by this one song." Speaking further of his songs, he says, "If there were in every town but three or four amateurs of both sexes who could sing them correctly, how many a happy hour and pleasant evening might be spent." His songs have been widely used in this and other countries; many of them having been introduced into this country by Dr. Lowell Mason in his school song books. He died in Zurich, Dec. 26, 1836.

Franz Schubert was born near Vienna, Jan. 31, 1797. At the age of eleven, having a fine voice, he was chosen as one of the boy-singers in the Court Chapel. He tried his hand at all forms of musical composition, but excelled in ballads and songs, in which he is hardly equalled. Among the more popular may be mentioned, "Erl King," "Serenade," "Last Greeting," "Post Horn," "Ave Maria," "Wanderer," etc. He died Nov. 19, 1828, and was buried near the grave of Beethoven in Wäbring, a suburb of Vienna.

Frederic Silcher, born in 1789, composed a large number of people's songs, and also made the first published collection of German Airs or Volkslieder.

Franz Abt, born in 1819, at Eilenburg, though still living, should be mentioned as one who has done much in the direction of Part Songs, of a moderately difficult character, for the people, many of them of great beauty, and should have a place in every collection of music, that they may become as "household words."

Mention might be made of Robert Schumann, Spohr, Rinck, Rossini, von Weber, Wagner, Gluck, Cherubini, and others, but space will not permit.

In a work of this educational character, however, mention should be made of one who would not rank, from a critical standpoint, with those mentioned above, as a composer, yet, who has doubtless done more than any one man, by his early gratuitous instructions to the young, and in the Boston schools, beginning in 1830, by his simple sacred and secular songs, composed and arranged from the German, and by his long-continued labors to elevate the standard of musical instruction throughout the land, to bring us as a nation up to our present musical status in appreciation and culture. The above statement would be recognized by the very many who have been permitted to enjoy his instruction, as referring to Dr. LOWELL MASON, who was born in Medfield, Mass., Jan. 8, 1792, and died in Orange, N. J., Aug. 11, 1872.

He rests from his labors, but the influence of them will never cease.

CHAPTER V.

An excellent occasional practice in Schools and Classes is to sing a Solfeggio or Song in unison. There are given here several Solfeggios in one, two, and three parts, and several Solos from Oratorios, which it is hoped will be useful.

No. 1. Base or Alto.

No. 2. Soprano or Tenor.

KUCKEN.

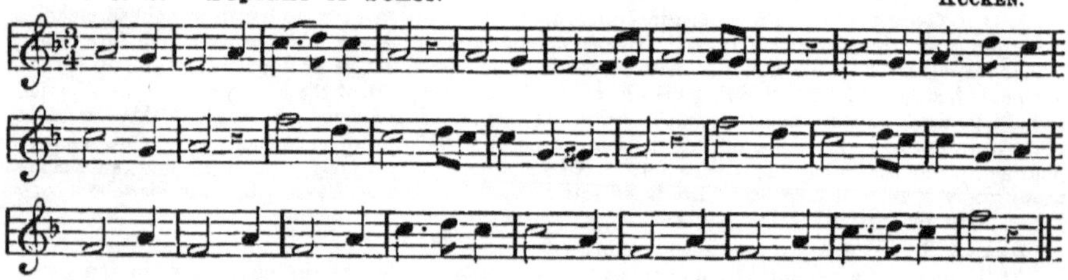

No. 3. Base or Alto.

No. 4. Soprano or Tenor.

T. COOKE.

SOLFEGGIOS. 35

No. 5. Base or Alto.

No. 6. Soprano or Tenor.   From OTTO.

No. 7. Base or Alto.

SOLFEGGIOS. 37

No. 11.   Soprano and Tenor may sing the upper part, and Alto and Base the lower.

MENDELSSOHN.

No. 12.   From CONCONE.

SOLFEGGIOS.

No. 13. From RHIGINI.

SOLFEGGIOS. 39

BUT THE LORD IS MINDFUL OF HIS OWN.

From MENDELSSOHN'S "ST. PAUL."

ALTO SOLO.

But the Lord is mind-ful of His own; He re - mem-bers His chil-dren; But the Lord is mind-ful of His own; The Lord re - mem-bers His

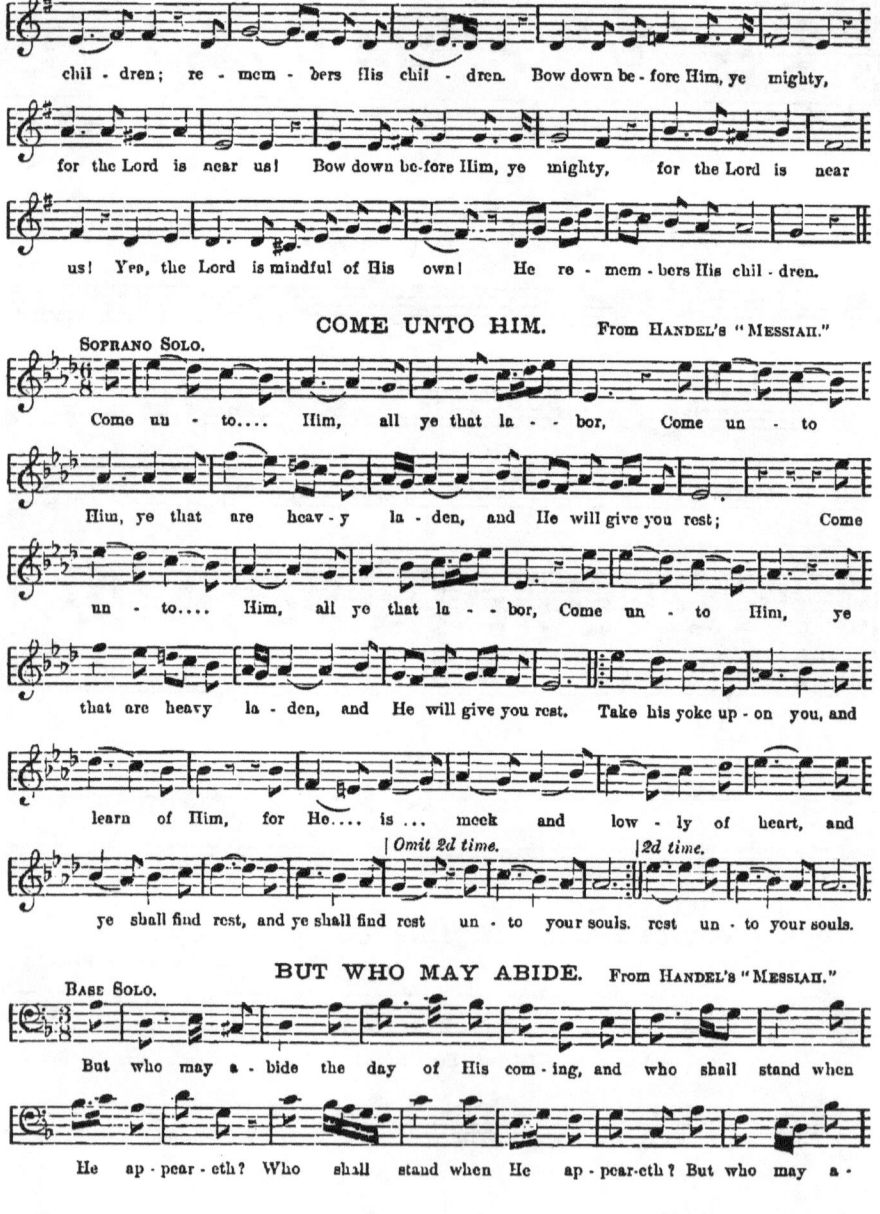

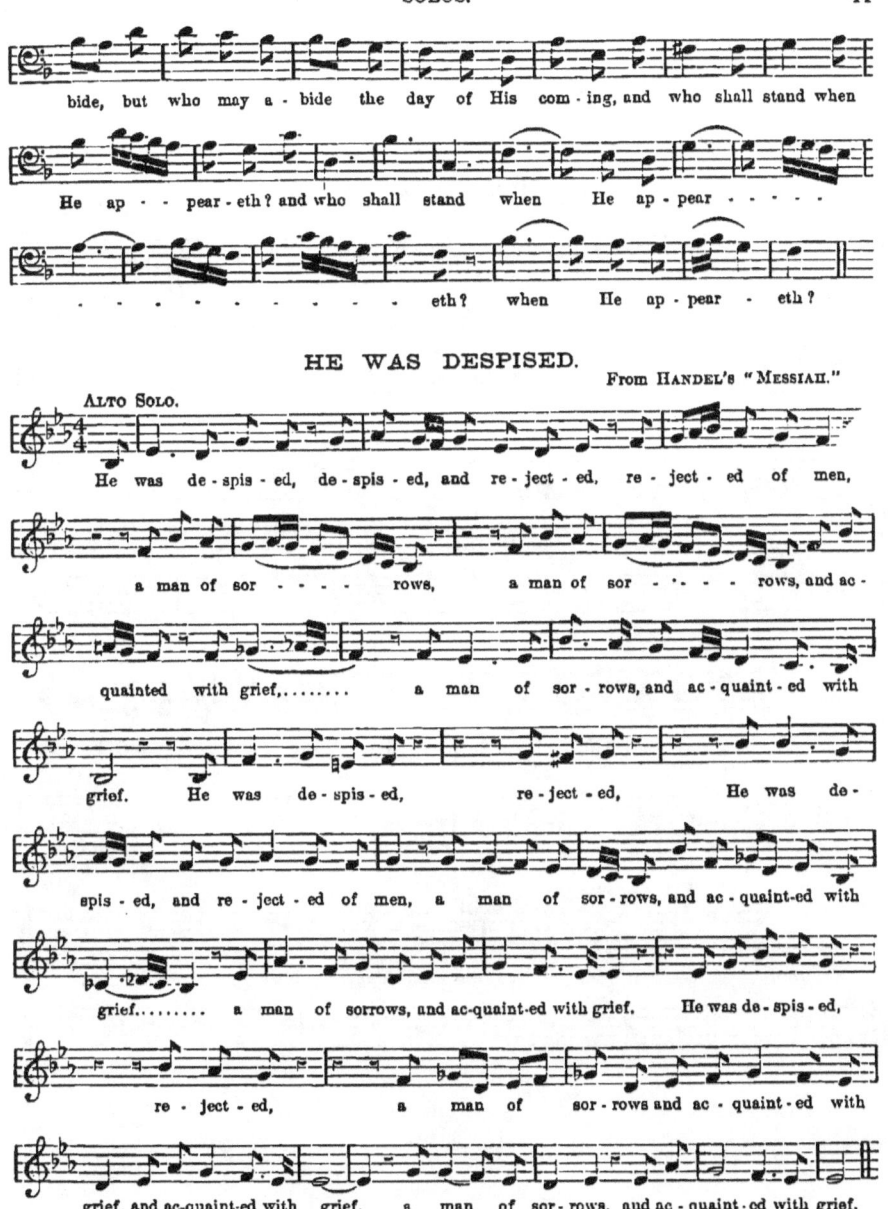

CHAPTER VI.

CONSISTING OF MUSIC IN ONE, TWO, AND THREE PARTS.

ARRANGED FOR SOPRANO, ALTO, AND BASE.

BEGONE, DULL CARE.

Old English.

MUSIC ON THE WAVES.

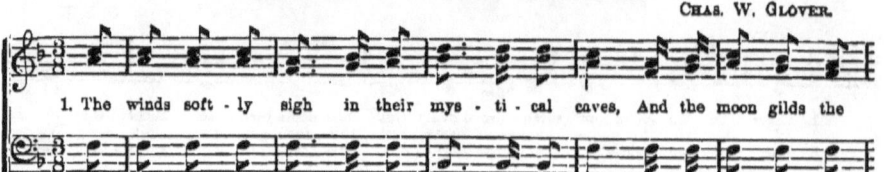

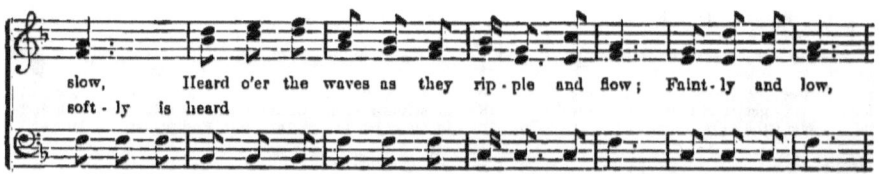

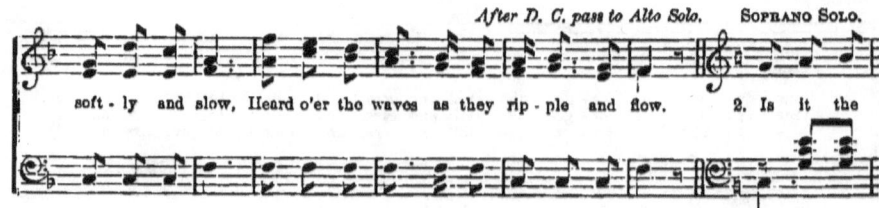

A SUMMER PICTURE.

Allegretto.

1. From saf-fron to pur-ple, from pur-ple to gray, Slow fades on the mountain the
2. Low sings the glad riv-er a-long its dark way, An ech-o by night of its
3. The dew glit-ters bright where the meadows are green, In ranks of white splen-dor the

beau-ti-ful day; I sit where the ro-ses are heav-y with bloom, And
chim-ing by day, And trem-u-lous branches lean down to the tide, To
lil-ies are seen; The ro-ses a-bove me sway light-ly to greet Their

wait for the moon-light to whit-en the gloom. Far down the green val-ley I
dim-ple the wa-ters that un-der them glide. I sit in the shadow, but
sha-dow-y sis-ters a-float at my feet. How sings the glad riv-er, its

see through the night, The lamps of the vil-lage shine steady and bright; But on my sweet
lo! in the west The mountains in gar-ments of glo-ry are drest! And slow-ly the
wa-ters a-light, A path-way of sil-ver lead on thro the night; And fair as the

si-lence there creeps not a tone Of la-bor or sor-row, of plead-ing or moan.
sheen of their brightness drops down, To rest on the hills in a lu-mi-nous crown.
glo-ri-fied Isles of the blest Lies all the sweet val-ley, the val-ley of rest.

THE SUN SMILES IN BEAUTY.

Welsh Air—"The Ash Grove."

OLD FRIENDS AND OLD TIMES.
51

way, Far, far a-way, Homes far a-way, Far, far a-way.
way, Far, far a-way, Friends far a-way, Far, far a-way.

Far a-way, Far a-way,

DREAM ON.

(In singing, the Tenor may be omitted.)   From the German.

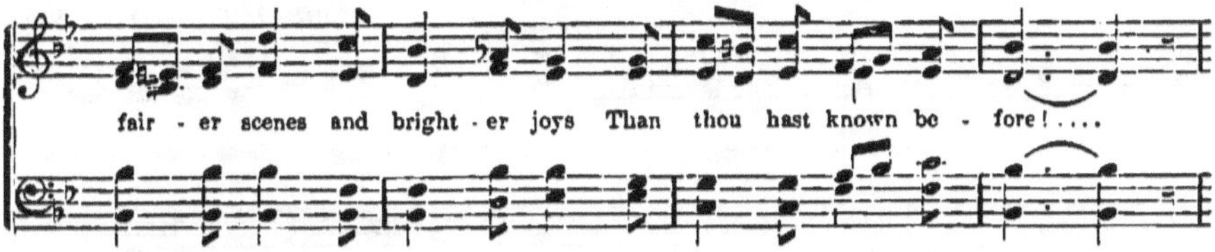

1. Dream on, young heart, of com-ing bliss The fu-ture has in store! Of fair-er scenes and bright-er joys Than thou hast known be-fore!.... Then dream.. on, dream on, dream on,.... dream on.....

2 To Hope's enchanting voice give ear,
   To her thy lot resign ;
What, though the scenes thy fancy paints
May never all be thine !
   Then dream on, dream on.

3 Or when the clouds grow dark above,
   And dangers dread proclaim ;
Still listen to the song of Hope,
And trust it all the same.
   Then dream on, dream on.

4 Dream on amid life's toils and cares,
   Whatever they may be !
'Twill make the burden lighter seem
That falleth here to thee.
   Then dream on, dream on.

5 But dream of joy, and not of woe,
   Thou'lt have enough of grief ;
Dream on of blessedness in store,
'Twill give thy heart relief.
   Then dream on, dream on.

WANDERING IN THE MAY-TIME

FAR DOWN IN YONDER VALE.

CHAPTER VII.

CONSISTING CHIEFLY OF FOUR-PART MUSIC ARRANGED FOR SOPRANO, ALTO, TENOR, AND BASE.

THE SEA.

W. WÜRFEL.

2. The sea, the summer sea!
There's nothing so bright as the sea!
When the rippling waters are glancing
In sunshine, like diamonds dancing,
Who does not but love the sea!
The dazzling summer sea!
    Hurrah, hurrah, hurrah!

3. The sea, the stormy sea!
The home of the brave and the free!
Each moment our spirits are rising,
While hardships and danger despising,
We sail on the stormy sea!
The wild, the stormy sea!
    Hurrah, hurrah, hurrah!

THE CURFEW.

From the German.

DUET. *Moderato.*

1. The cur-few is toll-ing the eve-ning knell, 'Tis the gray-head-ed sex-ton who pulls the bell; He rings and he rings, and you and I Love to loit-er and list-en in pass-ing by; He rings and he rings, and you and I Love to loit-er and list-en in pass-ing by.
2. The cur-few is toll'd for the close of the day, It is toll'd by that sex-ton so old and gray: Its knell, should it make us smile or sigh, As we loit-er and list-en in pass-ing by? Its knell, should it make us smile or sigh, As we loit-er and list-en in pass-ing by?
3. The gray-head-ed man, and the sol-emn chime, Re-mind us of death and the flight of time; They tell us of days we've spent in vain, And we sigh, but they will not come back a-gain; They tell us of days we've spent in vain, And we sigh, but they will not come back a-gain.

CHORUS.

1. Love to loit-er and list-en in pass-ing by, Love to loit-er and list-en in pass-ing by.
2. As we loit-er and list-en in pass-ing by, As we loit-er and list-en in pass-ing by?
3. And we sigh, but they will not come back a-gain, And we sigh, but they will not come back a-gain.

4 They ask us too if, as the night draws near,
  We can lie down to rest without doubt or fear?
  With peace in our hearts to close our eyes,
  And sleep till the dawning shall bid us rise.

5 The bell seems to say, like a warning voice,
  "While you loiter and listen, O make your choice!
  At night do you wish to smile or sigh,
  You must choose in the day, when the sun is high."

SPRING'S BRIGHT GLANCES. 69

WHEN THE LIGHT OF MEMORY.

71

Words written for this Work by E. R. LATTA.　　　　　　　　　*Bohemian Melody.*
Allegretto. p

1. When the light of mem-o-ry Brings back our child-ish joys, And re-stores the hap-py days When we were girls and boys; When our steps were free and light, And we knew naught of care; When we played our mer-ry games, And wander'd here and there! La, la, la, la, la, la, la, la, la, la, la, la, la, la, la,

2. When the light of mem-o-ry, As oft we sit a-lone, Fond-ly paints the fa-ces bright Of com-rades we have known; They who shared our ev-'ry ill (The lit-tle ills we knew), And par-took of all our joys, Those friends so warm and true!

3. When the light of mem-o-ry Doth on us bright-ly fall, Voi-ces of the loved we hear, And know each gen-tle call; Voi-ces that our hearts did thrill, With tones of mu-sic then, Sound-ing from the sun-ny past, A-wake the soul a-gain!

WHEN THE LIGHT OF MEMORY.

WHEN THE LIGHT OF MEMORY.

73

la, la, la, la, la, la, la, la, la, la, la, la, la, la, la, la.

la, la, la, la, la, la, la, la, la, la, la, la, la, la, la, la.

SONG OF THE VIOLET.

CHARLES JEFFERYS.   CHARLES W. GLOVER.

Andantino. p

1. I on-ly want a lit-tle nook In field or hedge-row wild, Where sun and show'r a-
2. The dew-drop comes to cher-ish me, And when the night grows long I know the lark will
3. The win-try hours with frost and sleet May bear a-way my bloom; But then I know the

like may fall On na-ture's hum-blest child. O let it be where I can see The
soon a-wake To greet the day with song; The rain up-on my breast may fall, But
spring will come And cheer the win-ter's gloom. And when its sun-shine to the earth A-

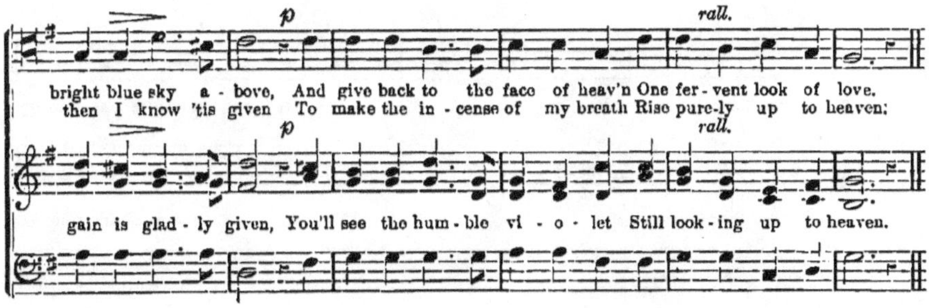

bright blue sky a-bove, And give back to the face of heav'n One fer-vent look of love.
then I know 'tis given To make the in-cense of my breath Rise pure-ly up to heaven;
gain is glad-ly given, You'll see the hum-ble vi-o-let Still look-ing up to heaven.

SEE HOW LIGHTLY ON THE BLUE SEA.

76. OH! 'TIS MERRY WHEN THE MOONBEAMS.

From "The Triad."
W. F. HEATH.

1. Oh! 'tis merry, merry, merry, Oh! 'tis merry when the moonbeams O'er the sparkling waters play, And a thousand stars are flashing From the billows' foaming spray.

1. Oh! 'tis sweet to hear the murmurs Stealing gently from the shores, When the melody is mingling With the music of the oars; O'er the billows sounding far,.. Hark! the shone, Speed thy bark, then, gaily on! Oh! 'tis merry when the moonbeams O'er the

2. I could fancy, in the ripple, That I see the Naiads play, While the siren mermaid cheers me With the magic of her lay. There is music in the sighing Of the

SOLO.

3. O'er the billows' roaming far... Come, then, with thy sweet guitar; Fairer night has never

OH! 'TIS MERRY WHEN THE MOONBEAMS.

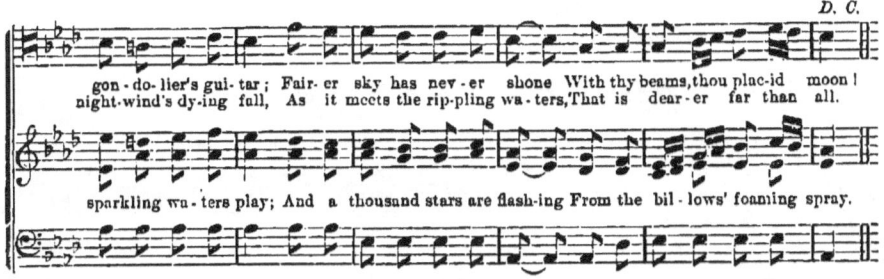

SUMMER SONG.

E. R. L.   *A Favorite Tyrolese Melody.*

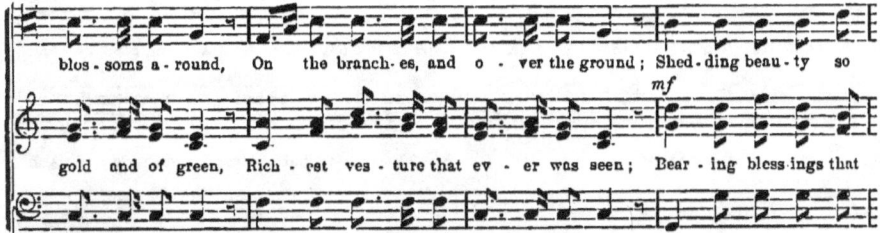

3 Summer fair! soothing our care!
Odors sweet fill the air!
Gentle showers, refreshing and cool,
Softly falling on meadow and pool;
Weaving fancies of pleasures flown,
Weaving with slumb'rous tone!

4 Summer dear! coming to cheer!
Welcome thou! welcome here!
Strains of beauty thy coming doth bring;
Countless songsters their melodies sing,
Bearing blessings that softly fall,
Blessings for one and all.

THE WANDERER'S SONG.

From A. FRANZ, *by* R. L. D. — F. E. FESCA (1729—1826).

Allegretto.

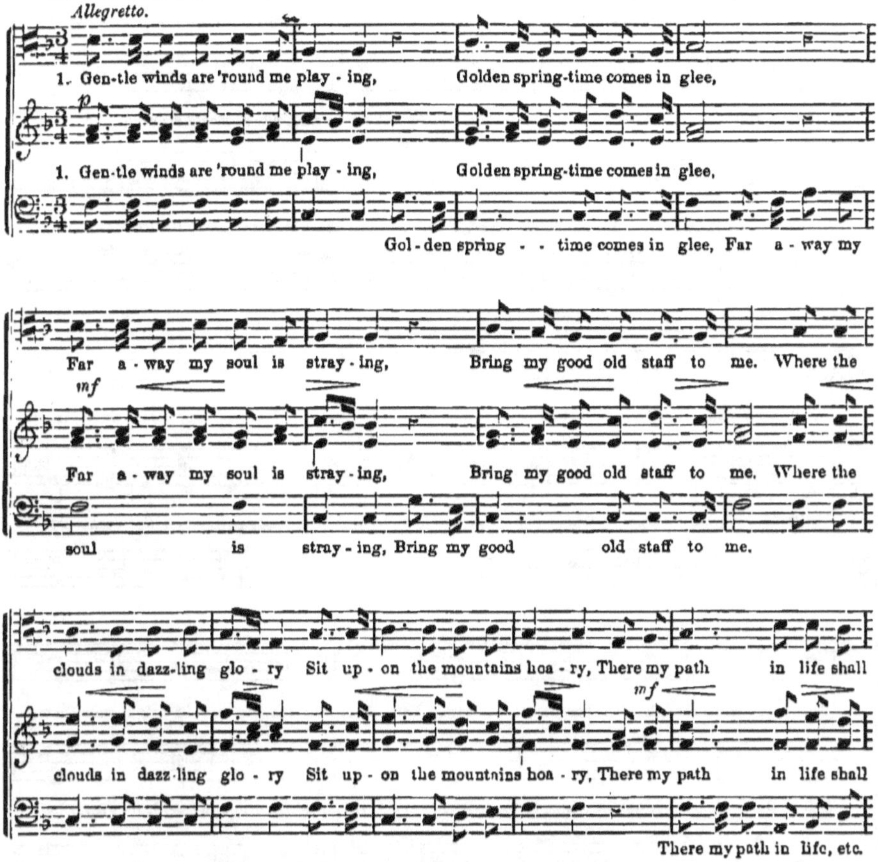

1. Gen-tle winds are 'round me play - ing, Golden spring-time comes in glee,
p
1. Gen-tle winds are 'round me play - ing, Golden spring-time comes in glee,
Gol - den spring - - time comes in glee, Far a - way my
Far a - way my soul is stray - ing, Bring my good old staff to me. Where the
mf
Far a - way my soul is stray - ing, Bring my good old staff to me. Where the
soul is stray - ing, Bring my good old staff to me.
clouds in dazz-ling glo - ry Sit up - on the mountains hoa - ry, There my path in life shall
mf
clouds in dazz-ling glo - ry Sit up - on the mountains hoa - ry, There my path in life shall
There my path in life, etc.

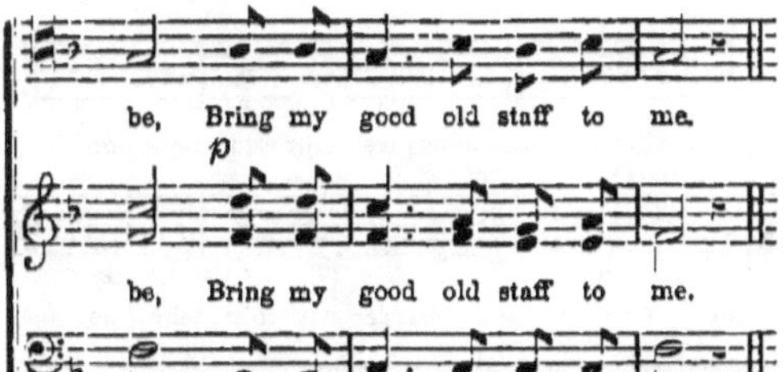

be, Bring my good old staff to me.
p
be, Bring my good old staff to me.

2. Fare you well, my way is yonder,
 Home shall never be forgot;
Fortune calls me now to wander,
 Full of hope I seek my lot.
Life from many fountains gushes,
Who would win to battle rushes;
Bold and free my feet must roam,
So farewell, my native home.

3. Near or far, may heaven love you,
 Still with you my heart shall stay;
When the sweet stars beam above you,
 Think of me, so far away.
On us all one sun is shining,
Let us part without repining;
Think of me when far away,
For with you my heart shall stay.

HERE WE REST.
FROM BELLINI'S "LA SONNAMBULA."

Words by CHARLES J. ROWE.   *Arranged by* EDWARD F. RIMBAULT.

TO-DAY AND TO-MORROW.

LESLIE WALTER.
Moderato.
BEETHOVEN (1770—1827). *Unaltered, from a set of songs, Op. 52.*

1. A rose-bud blossom'd in my bow'r, A bird sang in my garden; The rose-bud was its fair-est flow'r, The bird its gen-tlest war-den; And a child be-side the lin-den tree Sang, "Think no more of sor-row, But let us smile and sing to-day, For we must weep to-mor-row."

2. I ask'd the bird, "Oh, didst thou hear The song that she would sing thee? And can it be that thou wouldst fear What the next morn may bring thee?" He an-swer'd with tri-um-phant strain, And said, "I know not sor-row; But I must sing my best to-day, For I may die to-mor-row."

3. I ask'd the rose, "Oh, tell me, sweet, In thy first beau-ty's dawn-ing, Thou canst not fear from this re-treat The com-ing of the morn-ing?" She flung her fra-grant leaves a-part, The love-lier for her sor-row, And said, "Yet I must bloom to-day, For I may droop to-mor-row."

4.
I said, "The bloom upon my cheek
Is fleeting as the rose's ;
My voice no more shall sing or speak
When dust in dust reposes;
And from these soulless monitors
One lesson I may borrow,—
That we should smile and sing to-day,
For we may weep to-morrow."

THE HAPPY PEASANTS.

Air by Schumann.   *Arranged by* W. F. Taylor.

HYMN OF THE FISHERMEN'S CHILDREN.

Words by Charles J. Rowe.   *From* Herold's "*Zampa.*"   *Arr. by* Edward F. Rimbault.

HYMN OF THE FISHERMEN'S CHILDREN.

… sil-v'ry light, Then the chil-dren's voi ces rise, Blend-ing with the shades of night.

… storm-y night; Spare our moth-ers, on their knees, Watch-ing for the morn-ing light."

MEDITATION.

GOETHE. F. KUHLAU (1786—1832).
Andantino.

1. Un-der ev-ery hill-side is peace, And ev-ery bird is wrapt in its peace-ful nest; The leaf is scarce heard to rus-tle; Wait a-while, wait a-while, soon, ah! soon thou too shalt rest; Wait a-while, wait a-while, soon, ah! soon thou too shalt rest, soon thou too shalt rest.

2 Under every sky there is pain,
  And every day some signal of woe is made,
  The flowret fades and is withered;   [fade.
  Wait awhile, wait awhile, soon, ah! soon thou too shalt

3 Under every star there is rest,
  From every planet hear we soft music ring,
  The angels sing and they whisper,   [sing.
  Wait awhile, wait awhile, soon thou too our song shalt

THE ROBIN.

Eliza Cook.
Moderato.
S. Glover.

1. I wish I could welcome the spring, bonnie bird, With a carol as joyous as thine: Would my heart were as light as thy wing, bonnie bird, And thine eloquent spirit-song mine: You perch on the bud-cover'd spray, bonnie bird, O'er the turf where I chance to recline; And you sorrowful heaves That kept filling my eyes and my breath, When I wish I could welcome the spring, bonnie bird, With a carol as joyous as thine; Would my

2. I heard, in my childhood, the ballad that told Of the "snow coming down very fast," And the plaint of the robin, all starving and cold, Flung a spell that will live to the last. How my tiny heart struggled with

3. I sung to thee then as thou sing'st to me now, And my strain was as fresh and as wild; Oh!.. what is the laurel Fame twines for the brow To the wood-flowers plucked by the child? I wish I could welcome the

FAIRY MOONLIGHT.

GRADUATING SONG.

W. Locke Smith.

COME, COME AWAY!

FROM DONIZETTI'S "LA FAVORITE."

Words by CHARLES J. ROWE.   *Arranged by* EDWARD F. RIMBAULT.

SILENT NIGHT.

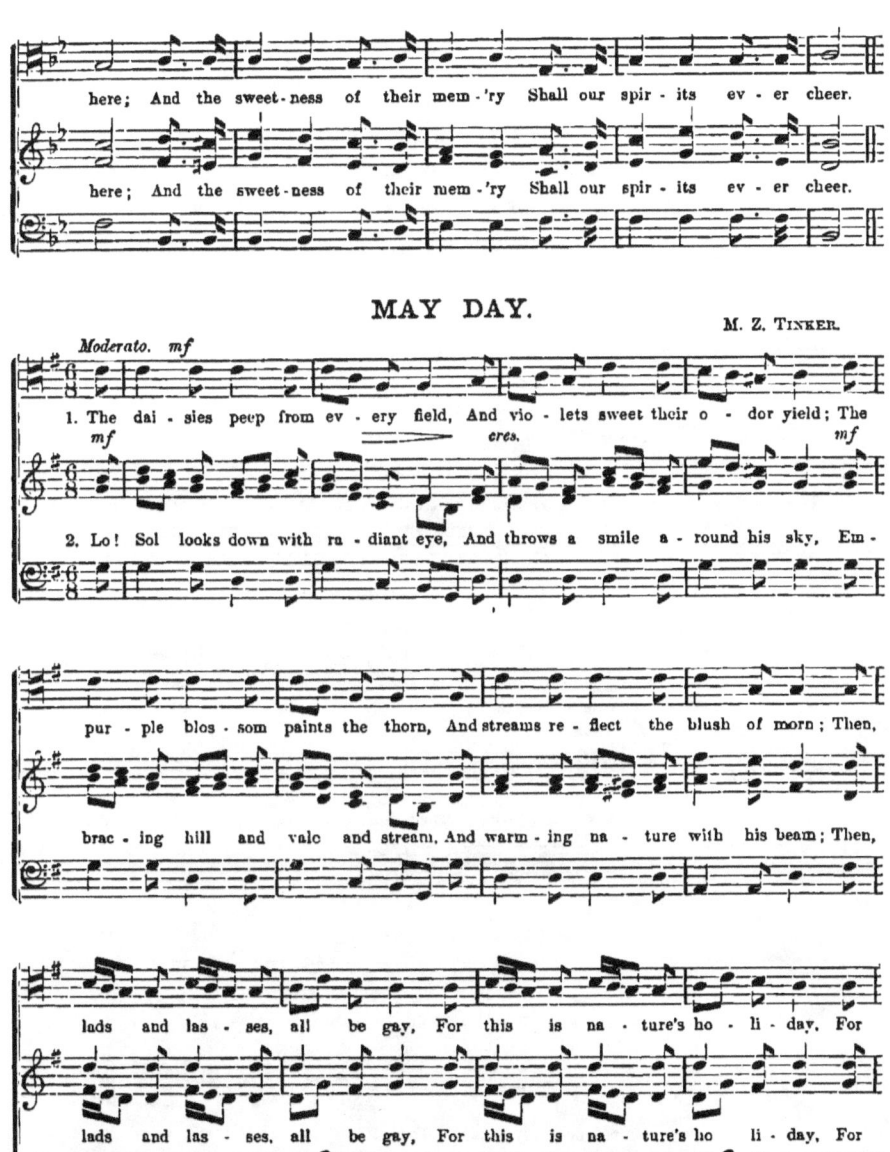

EVENING SONG.

THESE THINGS CAN NEVER DIE.

F. MULLER, *Vienna*.

AWAKE! THE DAYLIGHT SWEETLY FALLS.

greet the ope-ning day. Wake, a-wake, a-wake, Wake, a-wake, a-wake!
sedge-bird sings a-wake. Wake,........ a-wake, Wake, a-wake, a-wake!
thee my joy to share. Wake,........ a-wake, Wake,........ a-wake!

OUR CHILHOOD'S DAYS.

E. R. LATTA.   MOZART (1756—1791).
Allegretto.

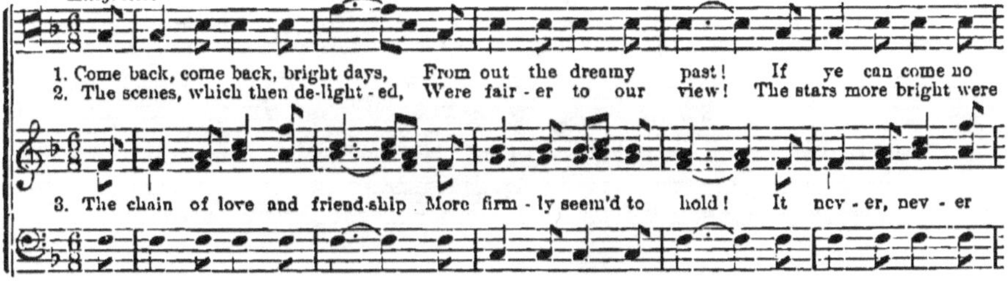

1. Come back, come back, bright days, From out the dreamy past! If ye can come no
2. The scenes, which then de-light-ed, Were fair-er to our view! The stars more bright were
3. The chain of love and friend-ship More firm-ly seem'd to hold! It nev-er, nev-er

more,.. Why did ye speed so fast? The days when we were chil - dren—How
gleam-ing! The skies ap-pear'd more blue! The days when we were chil - dren Up-
tarnished, Its links were pur-er gold! The days when we were chil - dren, De-

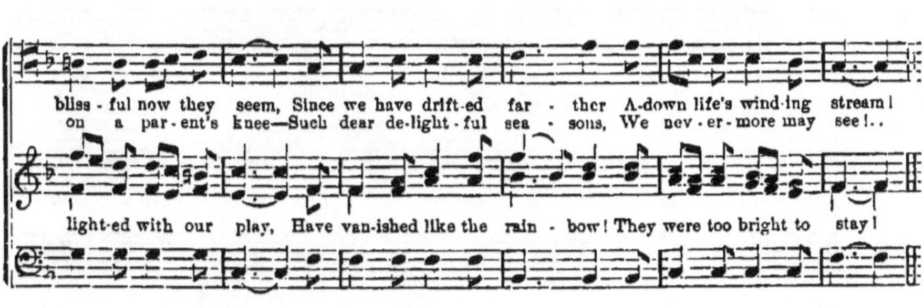

bliss-ful now they seem, Since we have drift-ed far - ther A-down life's wind-ing stream!
on a par-ent's knee—Such dear de-light-ful sea - sons, We nev-er-more may see!..
light-ed with our play, Have van-ished like the rain - bow! They were too bright to stay!

114

GOOD NIGHT.

GOOD NIGHT.

VOCAL WALTZ.

Words and Music by W. F. Taylor.

Note.—Should the fourth measure be found too difficult, the quarter rest and small G may be substituted for the four eighths in this and succeeding similar passages.

VOCAL WALTZ. 117

THE SPRING'S AWAKING.

From ROBERT KARWE, *by* R. L. D.
WILHELM BAADER.

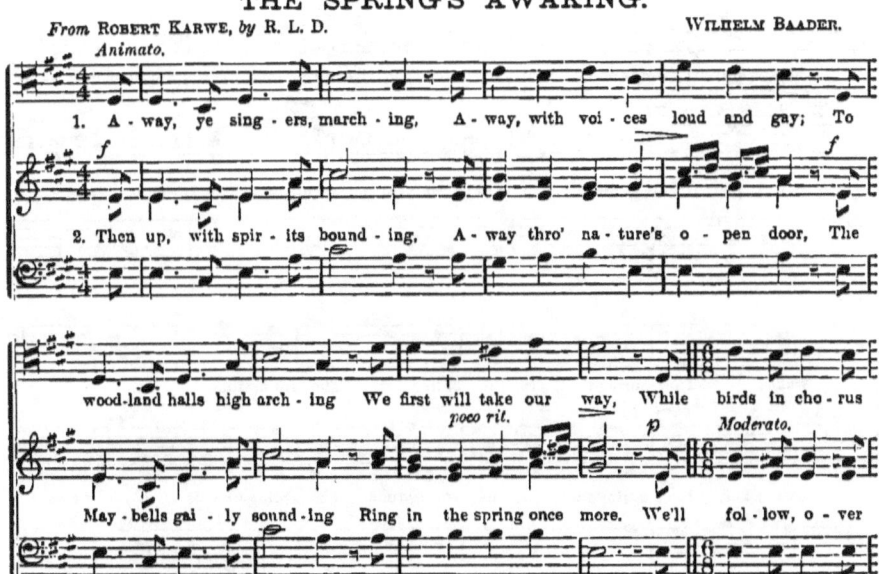

HENCE, NOW AWAY.

Allegro moderato.

LECOCQ.

1. Hence, now a-way to the bat-tle field, Faith, fear-less right is the war-rior's shield; Then peace once more will be smil-ing round, When back we come with lau-rels crown'd! Hence, now a-way to the bat-tle field, Faith, fear-less right is the war-rior's shield; Then peace once

2. To face the foe, brave war-riors, speed, A-bate their pride, reap hon-or's meed; Let coun-try's love our souls in-spire, And vir-tue's aim be our de-sire. To face the foe, brave war-riors, speed, A-bate their pride, reap hon-or's meed; Let coun-try's

THE ANGEL OF PATIENCE.

SPITTA.

3. He will not blame thy sorrows,
   But brings the healing balm;
   He does not chide thy longings,
   But soothes them into calm;
   And when thy heart is murm'ring,
   And wildly asking "Why?"
   He, smiling, beckons onward,
   And points unto the sky.

4. He will not always answer
   Thy questions and thy fear;
   His watchword is, "Be patient,
   The journey's end is near;"
   And ever through the toilsome way
   He tells of joys to come,
   And points to rest the pilgrim,
   The wand'rer to his home.

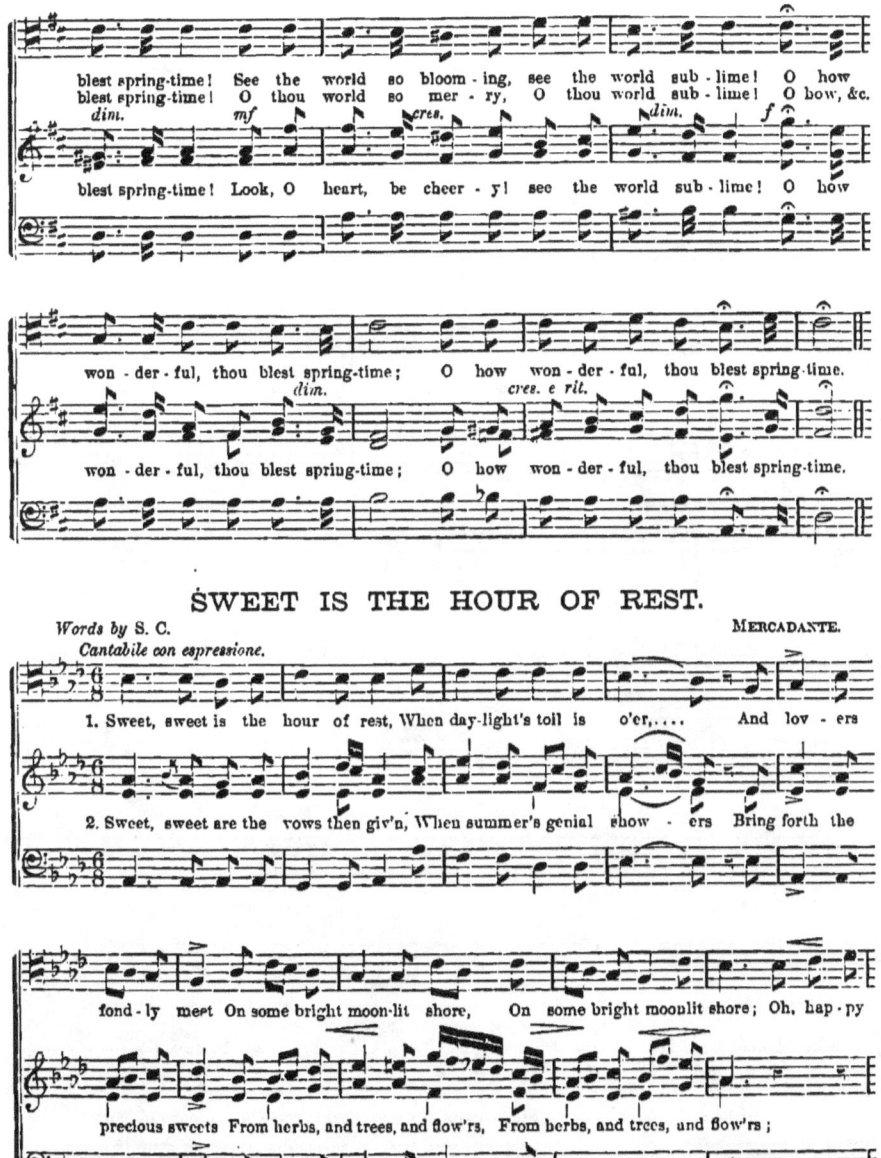

4 Then forgive and forget, if the friends we loved fondly
  Prove themselves to be false and unworthy of trust ;
  Oh ! deal with them kindly, for they are but mortals,
  And erring like us, for we too are but dust.
    Oh, forgive, etc.

5 Oh ! deal with them tenderly, pity their weakness,
  We know every heart has its evil and good ;
  We all have one Father in heaven, hence are brothers,
  Then let us forgive and forget as we should.
    Oh, forgive, etc.

FAYS AND ELVES.

ALPINE SHEPHERD'S SONG.

R. L. D.
Ferdinand Huber (1791—1863).

GOOD NIGHT.

From EMANUEL GEIBEL, *by* R. L. D.
Moderato.

FRANZ ABT (1819).

GOOD NIGHT.

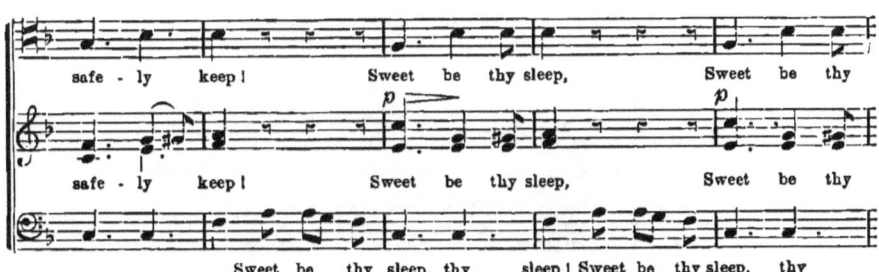

2 And now the lights have vanished,
   The darkness deeper grows,
All anxious thoughts are banished,
   That life in daylight knows.
From cypress branches stealing
There comes a blissful feeling,
   As soft the zephyr blows.
      Sweet be thy sleep, etc.

3 Good-night to every burden,
   To loved ones near and far,
Soon sleep shall be my guerdon
   Till beams the morning star.
High in the moonlight swinging,
The nightingale is singing,
   And these its warblings are:
      Sweet be thy sleep, etc.

COME, GENTLE MAY.

3 Come, vocal May! Come with thy warbling
  throng,
Pouring from field and grove their breathing song;
Carolling forth thy praise the live-long day,
In some lone glen retired, or echo calling,
Or 'mid the murm'ring woods, and dashing waters
  falling. Come, vocal May! &c.

4 Come, sunny May! Come with thy laughing
  beam;
Come when the mist is parting from the stream,
Seeking the mountain top, to meet thy ray,
Ere yet the dew-drop on thine own soft flower
Hath lost its diamond light, or died beneath his
  power. Come, sunny May! &c.

La, la, la, la, la, la, la, la, la, la, la, la, la.
pp
rit.
la, la, la, la, la, la, la, la, la, la, la, la, la.

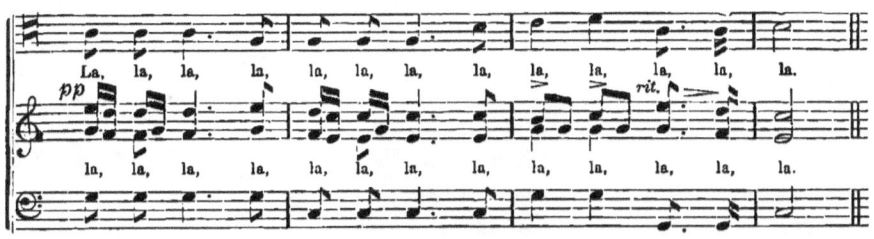

THE WELCOME SPRING.

E. R. Latta. Mendelssohn (1809—1847).

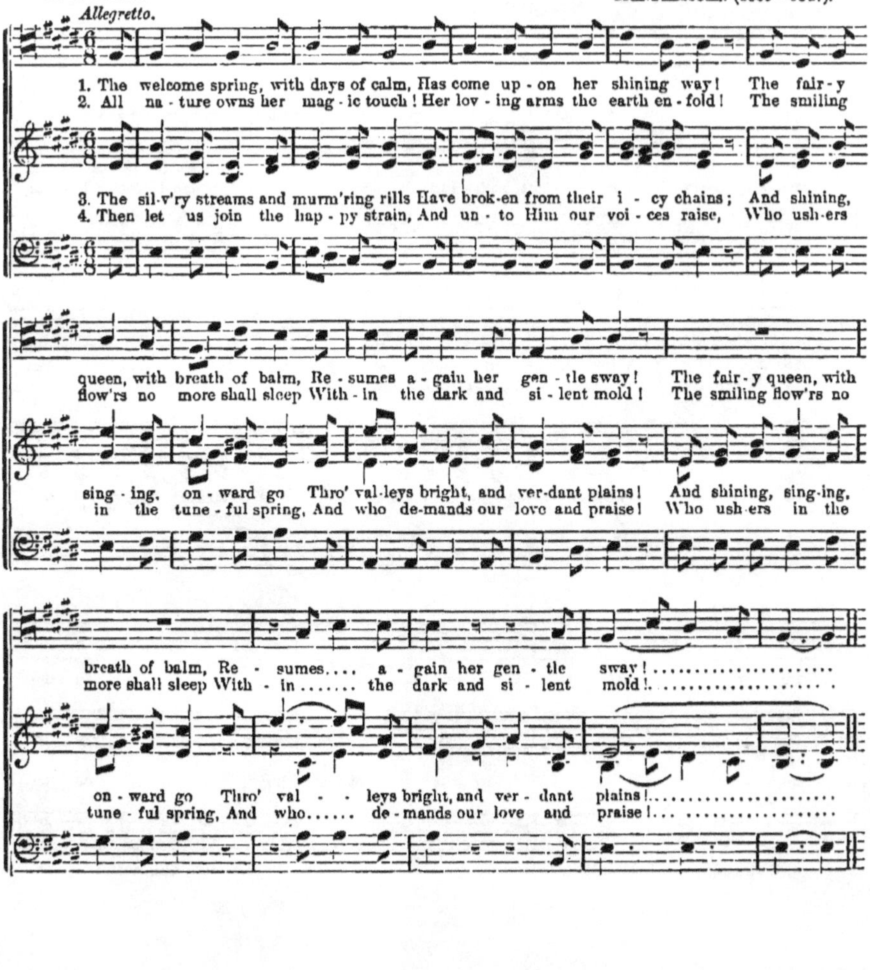
Allegretto.
1. The welcome spring, with days of calm, Has come up - on her shining way! The fair - y
2. All na - ture owns her mag - ic touch! Her lov - ing arms the earth en - fold! The smiling
3. The sil-v'ry streams and murm'ring rills Have brok-en from their i - cy chains; And shining,
4. Then let us join the hap - py strain, And un - to Him our voi - ces raise, Who ush-ers
queen, with breath of balm, Re - sumes a - gain her gen - tle sway! The fair - y queen, with
flow'rs no more shall sleep With - in the dark and si - lent mold! The smiling flow'rs no
sing - ing, on - ward go Thro' val-leys bright, and ver-dant plains! And shining, sing-ing,
in the tune - ful spring, And who de-mands our love and praise! Who ush-ers in the
breath of balm, Re - sumes.... a - gain her gen - tle sway!.......................
more shall sleep With - in....... the dark and si - lent mold!.......................
on - ward go Thro' val - - leys bright, and ver - dant plains!.......................
tune - ful spring, And who...... de - mands our love and praise!... ....

WHERE THE LOVED ONES WAIT.

Words by E. R. LATTA.   L. DE CALL.

WHERE THE LOVED ONES WAIT.

2 If, my friend, a home is thine,
  Dost thou prize it duly?
Are its inmates loved enough?
  Tell me, tell me truly!
In each pleasure, in each ill,
Strive to love them better still!
Watching, waiting still for thee,
  As the shades are falling!
Tenderly thy cherished name,
  Now I hear them calling.
Oh, how sad thy lot would be,
Did no loved ones wait for thee!

I KNOW NOT.   141

OH, BEAUTIFUL DREAMS.

E. R. L.
MENDELSSOHN (1809—1847).

Allegretto. mf

1. Oh, beau-ti-ful dreams Of mount-ains and streams, That haunt us while we are re-pos-ing! And re-al and true They seem to our view—Those vis-ions of beau-ty dis-clos-ing, Those vis-ions of beau-ty dis-clos-ing.

2. Oh, vis-ions so blest, When we are at rest, When in the still night we are sleep-ing; On pin-ions of light, With col-ors so bright, Ye in-to our pres-ence are sweep-ing, Ye in-to our pres-ence are sweep-ing.

OH, BEAUTIFUL DREAMS.

slum - bers ! . . Bright vis - ions pre - side o'er our slum - bers !
Bright vis - ions pre - side o'er our slum - bers !
mf cres. dim.
slum - bers ! . . Bright vis - ions pre - side o'er our slum - bers !
pre - side o'er our slum - bers !

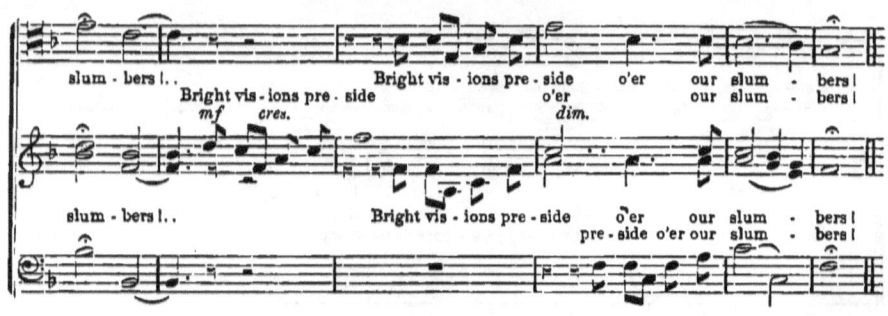

MARCH OF THE MEN OF HARLECH.

Words by WILLIAM DUTHIE. *Harmonized by* JOSEPH BARNBY.

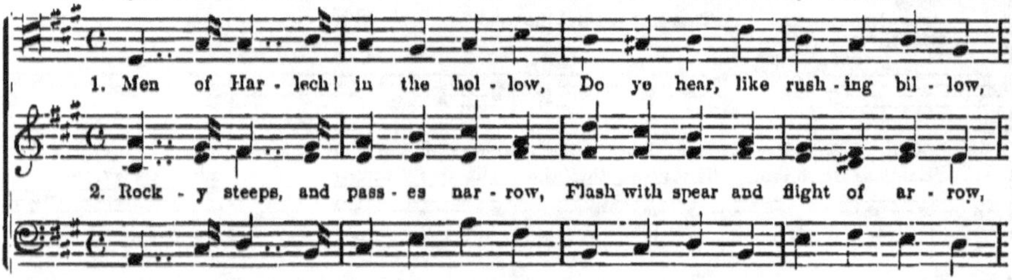
1. Men of Har - lech ! in the hol - low, Do ye hear, like rush - ing bil - low,
2. Rock - y steeps, and pass - es nar - row, Flash with spear and flight of ar - row,

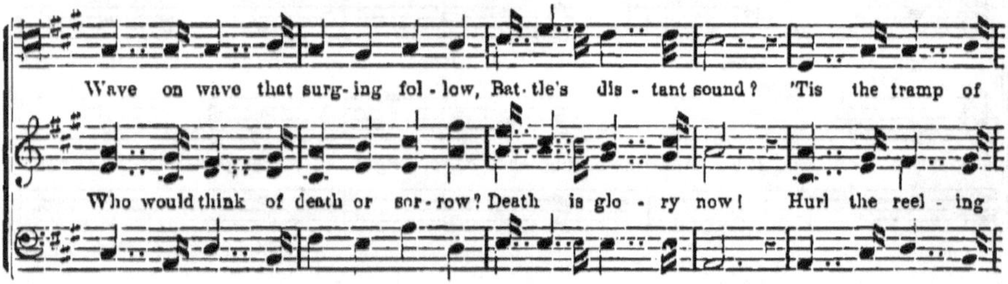
Wave on wave that surg - ing fol - low, Bat - tle's dis - tant sound ? 'Tis the tramp of
Who would think of death or sor - row ? Death is glo - ry now ! Hurl the reel - ing

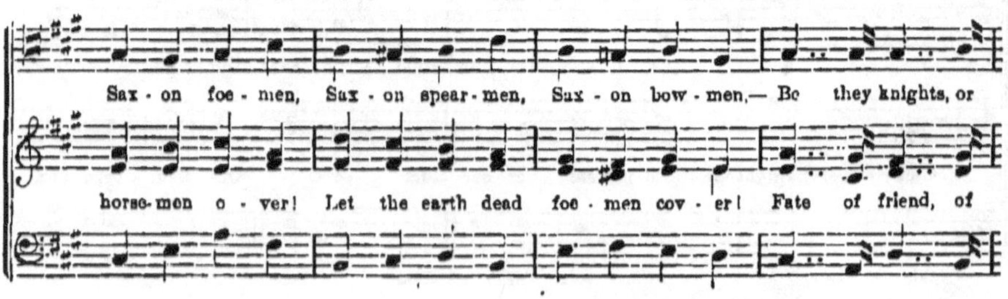
Sax - on foe - men, Sax - on spear - men, Sax - on bow - men,— Be they knights, or
horse - men o - ver ! Let the earth dead foe - men cov - er ! Fate of friend, of

MARCH OF THE MEN OF HARLECH.

146   **WHO WITH AN HONEST LOVE IS BLEST.**

From the German, by Miss Libbie Hamilton.   Carl Reinecke (1824).

THE VENETIAN BOATMEN'S EVENING SONG.

J. L. Hatton.

150 THE VENETIAN BOATMEN'S EVENING SONG.

Chorus.
O sa-cra, pi-a Vir-gi-ne,.... O-ra pro no-bis, O-ra pro
Sleeps in si-lence o-cean's queen.
She is pass-ing ev-er-more.

Solo.
Cho. O sa-cra, pi-a Vir-gi-ne,.... O-ra pro no-bis, O-ra pro

no-bis. O om-nes sa---cri An-ge--li,.... O-ra-te pro
no-bis. O om-nes sa---cri An-ge--li,.... O-ra-te pro

no-bis, O-ra-te pro no-bis, O sa-cra, pi--a
Hark! a-long the cur-rent glid-ing,
And to-night she seem-eth gaz-ing,
no-bis, O-ra-te pro no-bis. O sa-cra, pi--a

Vir---gi--ne, O-ra pro no--bis, O-ra pro
Boat-men chant their ves-per song, now chant their song, now chant their
Not a-lone up-on the sea, up--on the sea, up-on the
Vir---gi--ne,............ O-ra pro no-bis, O-ra pro

THE VENETIAN BOATMEN'S EVENING SONG.

no - bis. O om - nes sa - - - - cri An - ge - - li, ... O
song; While the evening's tran - - quil ze - - phyr
sea; But she seems with smil - - ing fea - - tures

no - bis. O om - nes sa - - - - cri An - ge - li, ... O

ra - te pro no - bis, O - ra - te pro no - bis. O sa - cra Vir - gi - ne,
Bears the swell - ing notes a - long, ...
Still be - hold - ing you and me, ...

ra - te pro no - bis, O - ra - te pro no - bis, O sa - cra Vir - gi - ne,

O.... om - nes An - ge - li, pro........ no - bis, pro no - - -
Bears the swelling notes a -
Still be-hold-ing you and

O.... om - nes An - ge - li, O - ra - te pro no - - bis, pro no - - -

bis, O - ra - te pro no - - bis, pro no - bis...............
long,......... the swell-ing notes a - long.............
me,............ be - hold - ing you and me...............
dim. al fine.

bis, O - ra - te pro no - - bis, pro no - bis...............

ON THE MOUNTAINS.

JOHANN WENZEL KALLIWODA (1801—1869.)

ON THE MOUNTAINS.

BALLAD OF THE WEAVER.

J. L. HATTON.

BALLAD OF THE WEAVER.

BALLAD OF THE WEAVER.

SERENADE SONG.

THE WATCH OF THE STARS.

From J. ALTMANN, *by* R. L. D.
EUGENE PIZOLD.

PHŒBUS.

round, the love-ly scene,.... the scene a - round. Phœbus shines in splendor
rall. p   *pp rit.*   *f a tempo.*
glade, throughout the glade,.... the wood-land glade. Phœbus shines in splendor
round, the love-ly scene a - round, the love-ly scene a - round.
glade, throughout the woodland glade, throughout the woodland glade.

o'er us, Let us thro' the meadows roam;.... Na-ture's face, so bright be -
p   f
o'er us, Let us thro' the meadows roam;.... Na-ture's face, so bright be -

fore us, Bids us wan-der from our home, Bids us wan - der from our home.
p   *cresc.*   f   *rit.*
fore us, Bids us wan-der from our home, Bids us wan - der from our home.

THE EARTH IS BEAUTIFUL.

Composed for this Work by WM. H. CLARKE.

Andantino.

1. This earth is ver - y beau - ti - ful When hearts are true and kind;.. If we but search for
2. How oft - en, too, a lit - tle word, Or kind - ly lov - ing thought, Is treasured deep with-
3. The beauteous scenes with which the earth Is man-tled ev - 'ry - where, Are but the shadows

THE EARTH IS BEAUTIFUL.

THE BANNER OF THE FREE.
A PATRIOTIC SONG.

169

Words by E. R. LATTA. Music by BRINLEY RICHARDS.

174. LIST! THE TRUMPET'S THRILLING SOUND.

Arranged from MEYERBEER, *by* W. H. BIRCH.

THE CHAPEL.

UHLAND. KREUTZER.

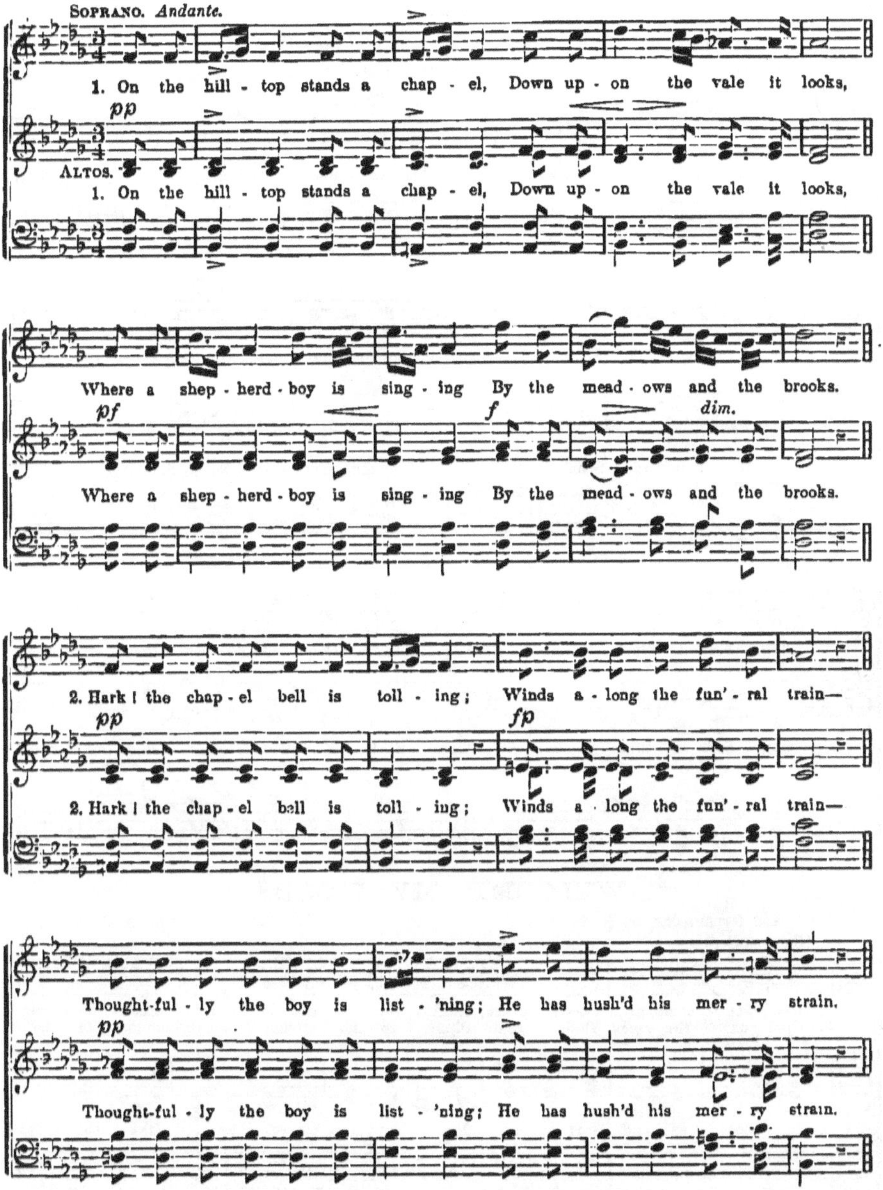
SOPRANO. Andante.
1. On the hill-top stands a chapel, Down upon the vale it looks,
pp
ALTOS.
1. On the hill-top stands a chapel, Down upon the vale it looks,
Where a shep-herd-boy is sing-ing By the mead-ows and the brooks.
pf
f
dim.
Where a shep-herd-boy is sing-ing By the mead-ows and the brooks.
2. Hark! the chap-el bell is toll-ing; Winds a-long the fun'-ral train—
pp
fp
2. Hark! the chap-el bell is toll-ing; Winds a-long the fun'-ral train—
Thought-ful-ly the boy is list-'ning; He has hush'd his mer-ry strain.
pp
Thought-ful-ly the boy is list-'ning; He has hush'd his mer-ry strain.

WELCOME, MY WOODS.

3.

He lived through the whole of the thousand years
    Of Rome's imperial pride;
He saw all her thrones and he saw her biers,
    And her kings that lived and died!
He bore up aloft the poor martyr's prayer,
    And the warrior's failing breath;
He has kissed the soft cheeks all blooming fair,
    And the cold icy lips of death!
He has lived through the years when time was young,
    In the ages so far away.

4.

He touches the lyres in the forest woods,
    The keys of a thousand plains;
And through all of the wide world's lone solitudes
    He awakens sweet refrains;
Their sweet cadences will still something be,
    When old time is known no more;
For he lived, yes, he lived when time began—
    He will live when old time is o'er!
For he'll live through the years when time is o'er,
    In the ages so far away.

THE OLD MAN.

FRANCIS JOSEPH HAYDN (1732—1809).
Composed near the close of his eventful life.

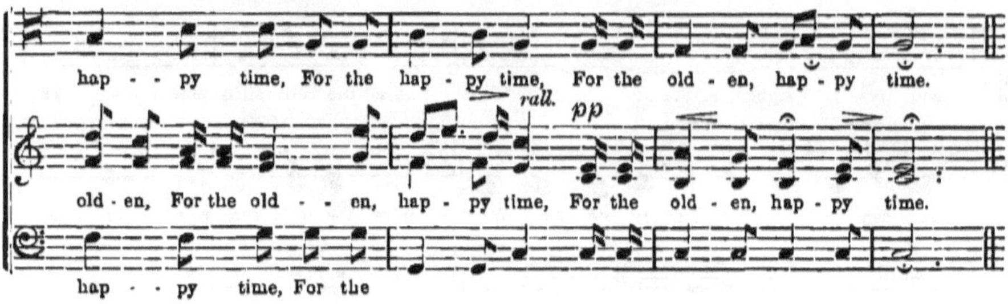

NIGHT, THOU HOLY NIGHT.

E. R. L.
Moderato.
Chwatal.

1. Night, O night, thou ho-ly night! Meadow, lake and woodland o-ver, Thou dost spread thy sa-ble cov-er; Sweet, sweet rest thou'rt wafting on So kind-ly to each wea-ry one! Sweet, sweet rest thou'rt waft-ing on So kind-ly to each wea-ry one!

2. Night, O night, thou ho-ly night! Thou dost bear us, in our dreaming, Up thro' scenes more bright-ly gleaming, Lead'st us smil-ing to suc-cess; Oh! turn us not from hap-pi-ness! Lead'st us smil-ing to suc-cess; Oh! turn us not from hap-pi-ness!

3. Night, O night, thou ho-ly night! In thine arms let me be rest-ing, Aft-er cares so long mo-lest-ing, Kind and faith-ful bring to me Sweet dreams while sleeping peace-ful-ly Kind and faith-ful bring to me Sweet dreams while sleep-ing peace-ful-ly!

THE PRIMROSE.

MENDELSSOHN (1809—1847).

THE NIGHTINGALE.

Words by E. R. Latta.
Moderato. p
Mendelssohn.

THE NIGHTINGALE.

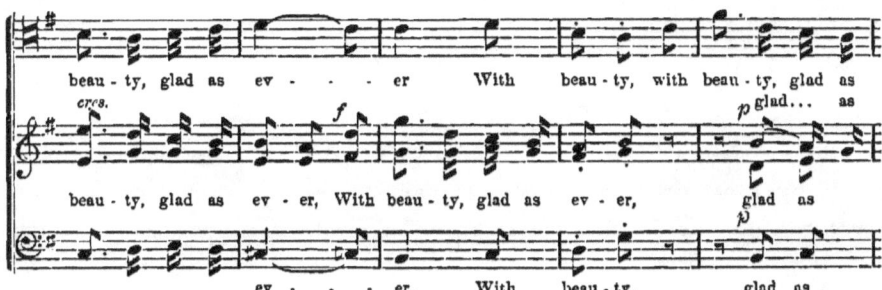

2 At her return, the burdened heart
   Methinks must beat more lightly;
 The features dark with clouds of care
   Must surely glow more brightly!
O nightingale, we love thy song,
   Thou ever-welcome comer!
How could we do without thy lay,
   In spring-time and in summer.

3 O nightingale, dear nightingale,
   In vain our hearts have sought thee;
 But now thou art our own again,
   The merry spring hath brought thee.
Oh, welcome back, dear nightingale,
   O'er field and lake and river!
If thou wouldst only stay with us,
   We'd keep thee here forever.

'TIS THE EVENING'S HOLY HOUR.

E. R. L.
L. V. Beethoven (1770—1827)

THE DAWNING OF THE DAY.

EARLY MORNING.

Arranged for this Work from KREUTZER (1783—1849).

EARLY MORNING.

201

'TIS THE LAST ROSE OF SUMMER.

Irish Air.

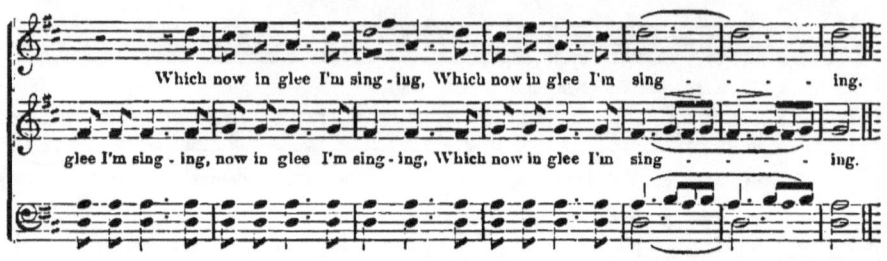

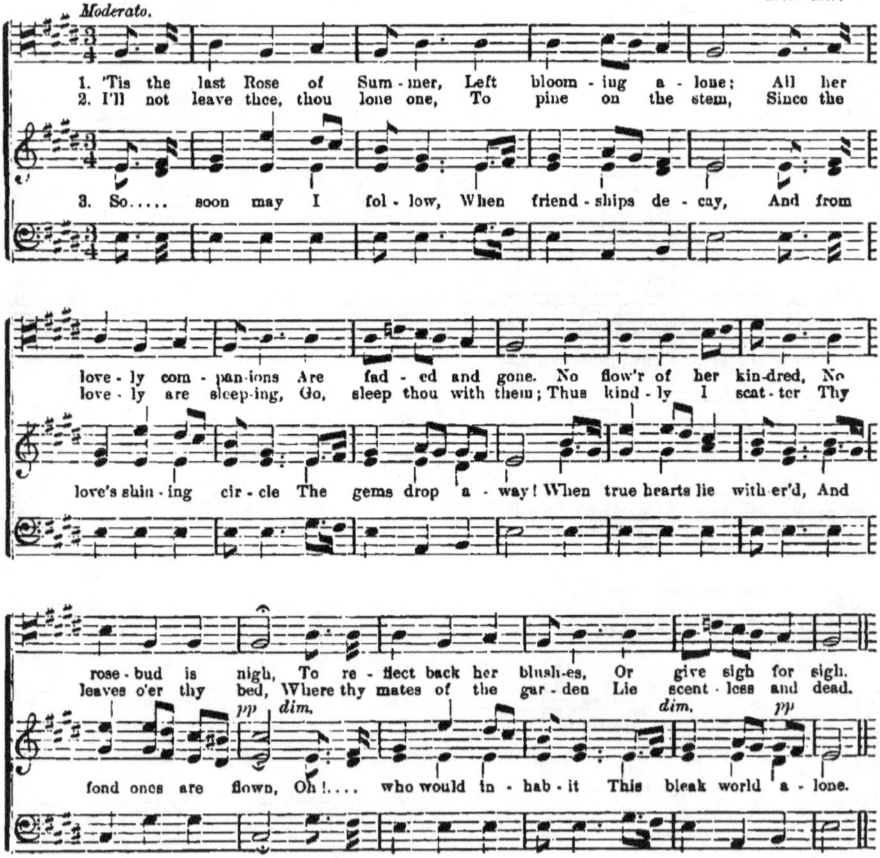

EARLY SPRING.

MENDELSSOHN (1809—1847).

206 PROTECT US THROUGH THE COMING NIGHT.

ADVENT OF SPRING.

Arranged for this work. CURSCHMANN (1805—1841).

CHAPTER VIII.

CONSISTING PRINCIPALLY OF DEVOTIONAL SONGS AND CHORUSES.

OLD HUNDRED.

W. Franc, 1543.

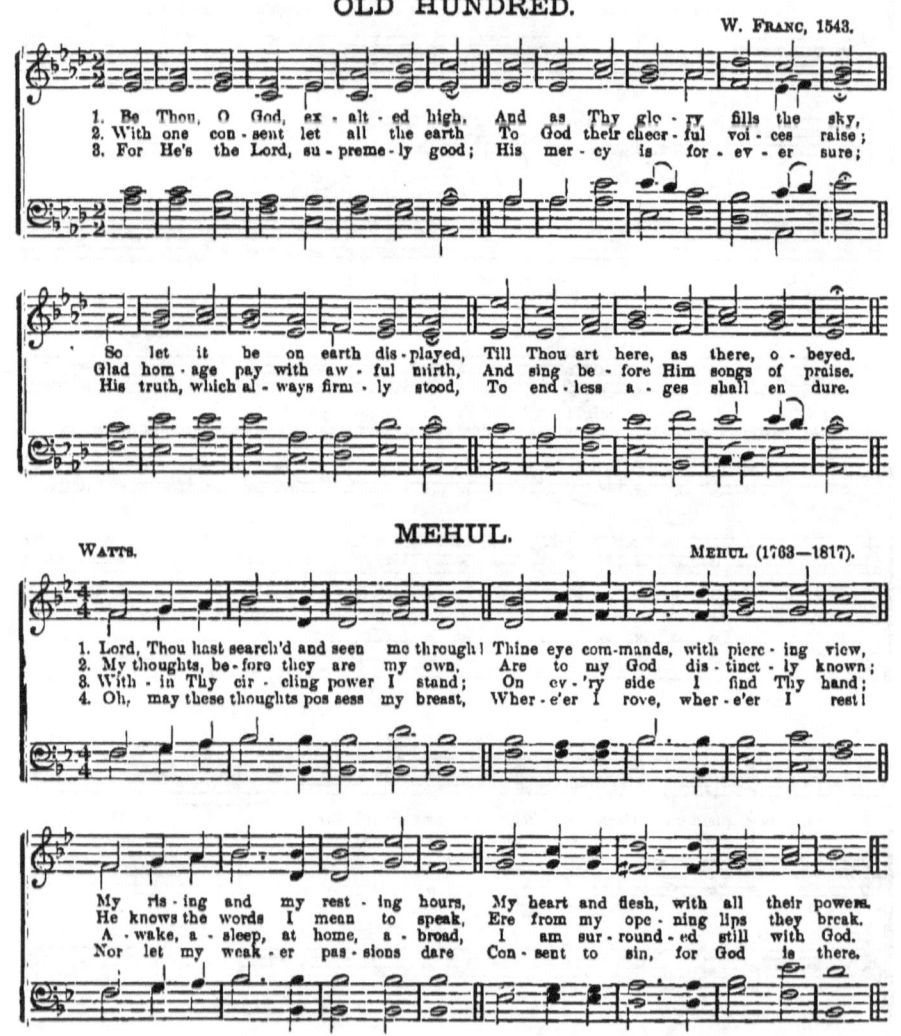

1. Be Thou, O God, ex-alt-ed high, And as Thy glo-ry fills the sky,
2. With one con-sent let all the earth To God their cheer-ful voi-ces raise;
3. For He's the Lord, su-preme-ly good; His mer-cy is for-ev-er sure;

So let it be on earth dis-played, Till Thou art here, as there, o-beyed.
Glad hom-age pay with aw-ful mirth, And sing be-fore Him songs of praise.
His truth, which al-ways firm-ly stood, To end-less a-ges shall en-dure.

MEHUL.

Watts.　　　　　　　　　　　　　　　　　Mehul (1763—1817).

1. Lord, Thou hast search'd and seen me through! Thine eye com-mands, with pierc-ing view,
2. My thoughts, be-fore they are my own, Are to my God dis-tinct-ly known;
3. With-in Thy cir-cling power I stand; On ev-'ry side I find Thy hand;
4. Oh, may these thoughts pos-sess my breast, Wher-e'er I rove, wher-e'er I rest!

My ris-ing and my rest-ing hours, My heart and flesh, with all their powers.
He knows the words I mean to speak, Ere from my ope-ning lips they break.
A-wake, a-sleep, at home, a-broad, I am sur-round-ed still with God.
Nor let my weak-er pas-sions dare Con-sent to sin, for God is there.

TUNE—"*America.*"

1 THE God of harvest praise ;
   In loud thanksgiving raise
      Hand, heart, and voice !
   The valleys laugh and sing ;
   Forests and mountains ring ;
   The plains their tribute bring ;
      The streams rejoice.
2 Yea, bless His holy name,
   And joyous thanks proclaim
      Through all the earth ;
   To glory in your lot
   Is comely ; but be not
   God's benefits forgot
      Amid your mirth.
3 The God of harvest praise ;
   Hands, hearts, and voices raise
      With sweet accord ;
   From field to garner throng,
   Bearing your sheaves along,
   And in your harvest song
      Bless ye the Lord.

TUNE—"*Italian Hymn.*"

1 PRAISE ye Jehovah's name,
   Praise through His courts proclaim ;
      Rise and adore ;
   High o'er the heavens above
   Sound His great acts of love,
   While His rich grace we prove
      Vast as His power.
2 Now let the trumpet raise
   Sounds of triumphant praise
      Wide as His fame :
   Then let the harp be found ;
   Organs, with solemn sound,
   Roll your deep notes around,
      Filled with His name.
3 While His high praise ye sing,
   Strike every sounding string,
      Sweet the accord !
   He vital breath bestows ;
   Let every breath that flows
   His noblest fame disclose :
      Praise ye the Lord.

AMELIA.

FATHER, TAKE MY HAND AND LEAD ME!

1 FATHER, take my hand and lead me,
  Hold it ever close in Thine;
Let Thy tender care provide me,
  Fill my soul with peace divine.
Thou art strong in loving-kindness,
  I am weak as man may be;
All my knowledge is but blindness,—
  Bright the light that shines in Thee.

2 Oh, do Thou in love befriend me,
  Let me feel Thee ever near;
What though sorrows may attend me,
  I shall neither fail nor fear.
Take my hand, and blessing, teaching,
  Loving mercy to me show,
Then Thy help and strength possessing,
  Where Thou leadest, I will go.

MESSIAH.

LOGAN.
Moderato.
GEORGE FREDERICK HANDEL (1685—1759).

1. Oh, happy is the man that hears Instruction's warning voice; And who celestial wisdom makes His early, only choice.
2. For she hath treasures greater far Than east and west unfold; And her rewards more precious are Than all their stores of gold.

3 She guides the young with innocence
  In pleasure's paths to tread ;
  A crown of glory she bestows
  Upon the hoary head.

4 According as her labors rise,
  So her rewards increase ;
  Her ways are ways of pleasantness,
  And all her paths are peace.

MONTGOMERY.
Allegretto.
PRAISE.
From MOZART (1756—1791).

1. All ye nations, praise the Lord; All ye lands, your voices raise; Heaven and earth, with loud accord, Praise the Lord, forever praise.
2. For His truth and mercy stand, Past, and present, and to be, Like the years.. of His right hand, Like His own eternity.
3. Praise Him, ye who know His love; Praise Him from the depths beneath; Praise Him in .... the heights above; Praise your Maker, all that breathe.

BARBAULD.
PRAISE TO GOD.
Tune—"PRAISE."

1 PRAISE to God, immortal praise,
  For the love that crowns our days ;
  Bounteous Source of every joy !
  Let Thy praise our tongues employ

2 For the blessings of the field,
  For the stores the gardens yield ;
  For the fruits in full supply,
  Ripened 'neath the summer sky.

3 All that spring with bounteous hand
  Scatters o'er the smiling land ;
  All that liberal autumn pours
  From her rich o'erflowing stores ;

4 These, great God, to Thee we owe,
  Source whence all our blessings flow ;
  And, for these, our souls shall raise
  Grateful vows, and solemn praise.

CHANTS.

SEVERAL Selections for Chanting are here given. Chanting differs from *singing* in not having a regular rhythmic movement, and from *speaking*, in having definite pitches. The words should be given with the distinctness and deliberation with which a good reader would read them.

CHANT. No. 1. TALLIS.   CHANT. No. 2.   DR. TURNER.

SELECTION 1.—Ps. 23.

1 The Lord | is my | shepherd ;
 I | shall — | not — | want.
2 He maketh me to lie down in | green — | pastures ;
 He leadeth me be- | side the | still — | waters.
3 He re- | storeth my | soul :
 He leadeth me in the paths of righteousness | for His | name's — | sake.
4 Yea, though I walk through the valley of the shadow of death, I will | fear no | evil :
 For Thou art with me; Thy rod and Thy | staff they | comfort | me.
5 Thou preparest a table before me in the presence | of mine | enemies.
 Thou anointest my head with oil ; my | cup — | runneth | over.
6 Surely goodness and mercy shall follow me all the | days of my | life ;
 And I will dwell in the | house of the | Lord for | ever.

SELECTION 2.—Ps. 67.

1 God be merciful unto | us, and | bless us ;
 And cause His | face to | shine up-on | us.
2 That Thy way may be | known up-on | earth,
 Thy saving | health a- | mong all | nations.
3 Let the people praise | Thee, O | God ;
 Let | all the | people | praise Thee.

4 Oh, let the nations be glad and | sing for | joy ;
 For Thou shalt judge the people righteously, and govern the | nations | upon | earth.
5 Let the people praise | Thee, O | God ;
 Let | all the | people | praise Thee.
6 Then shall the earth | yield her | increase ;
 And God, even | our own | God, shall | bless us.
7 God | shall — | bless us ;
 And all the ends of the | earth shall | fear — | Him.

SELECTION 3.—Ps. 121.

1 I will lift up mine eyes | unto the | hills,
 From | whence — | cometh my | help.
2 My help cometh | from the | Lord,
 Who | made — | heaven and | earth.
3 He will not suffer thy | foot to be | mov-ed,
 He that | keepeth thee | will not | slumber.
4 Behold, He that keepeth | Isra- | el
 Shall neither | slumber | nor — | sleep.
5 The Lord | is thy | keeper :
 The Lord is thy shade up- | on thy | right — | hand.
6 The sun shall not | smite thee by | day,
 Nor the | moon — | by — | night.
7 The Lord shall preserve thee from | all — | evil ;
 He | shall pre- | serve thy | soul.
8 The Lord shall preserve thy going out and thy | coming | in,
 From this time forth, and | even for | ever- | more

RESPONSIVE CHANT. No. 3.

THE LEAD.—*To be sung by a single voice.*   THE RESPONSE—*To be sung by all.*   *After last verse.*

A - men.

SELECTION 4.—Ps. 136.

Lead. 1 Oh, give thanks unto the Lord, for | He is | good :
 Response. For His | mercy en- | dureth for | ever.
 (*This response is to be repeated at every verse.*)
2 Oh, give thanks unto the | God of | gods :
3 Oh, give thanks to the | Lord of | lords :
4 To Him who alone | doeth great | wonders :
5 To Him that by wisdom | made the | heavens :
6 To Him that stretched out the earth a- | bove the | waters ;
7 To Him that | made great | lights :
8 The sun to | rule by | day :
9 The moon and stars to | rule by | night :
10 Who remembered us in our | low es- | tate :
11 And hath redeem-ed us | from our | enemies :
12 Who giveth food to | all —| flesh :
13 Oh, give thanks unto the | God of | heaven :

BE STILL IN GOD.

From Julius Sturm.
Moderato.

1. Be still in God! Who rests on Him En-dur-ing peace shall know, And with a spir-it fresh and free Thro' life shall cheer-ly go. Be still in faith! For-bear to seek Wher seek-ing naught a-vails; Un-fold thy soul to that pure light From heav'n, which never fails. Un-fold thy soul to that pure light From heav'n, which nev-er fails.

2. Be still in love! Be like the dew That, fall-ing from the skies, On meadows green, in thous-and cups, At morn-ing twinkling lies! Be still in con-duct, striv-ing not For hon-or, wealth or might! Who in con-tent-ment breaks his bread Finds fa-vor in God's sight; Who in con-tent-ment breaks his bread Finds fa-vor in God's sight.

3. Be still in sor-row! "As God wills!" Let that thy mot-to be; Sub-mis-sive 'neath His strokes re-ceive His im-age stamped on thee. Be still in God! Who rests on Him En-dur-ing peace shall know, And with a spir-it glad and free Thro' night and grief shall go; And with a spir-it glad and free Thro' night and grief shall go.

MORNING PRAYER.

217

R. L. D.
Moderato.

JOSEPH HAYDN (1732—1809).

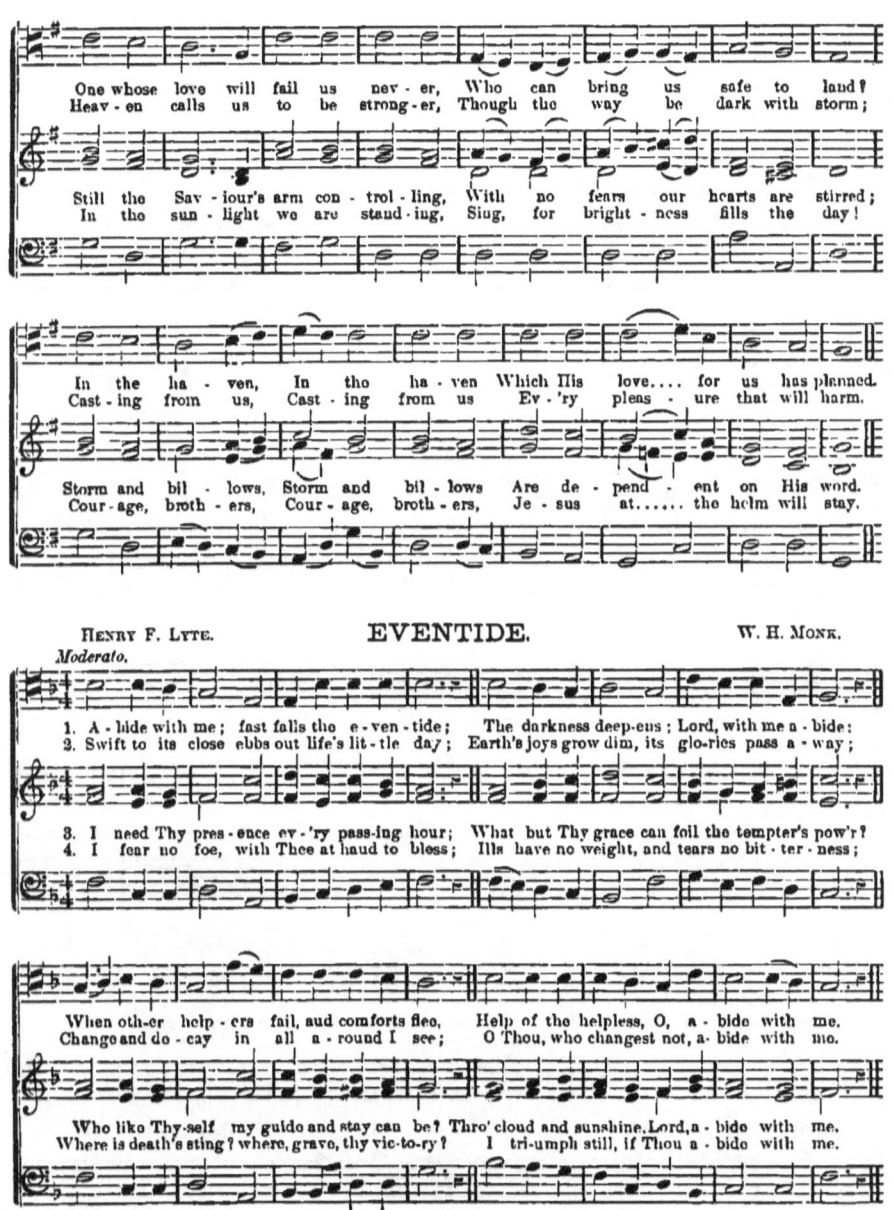

ROUSE THEE, O MY SPIRIT.

R. L. D.
Spiritoso.
Cæsar Malan (1786—1847).

1st time, Quartette; 2d time, Chorus.

1. Rouse thee, O my spir-it, Stay not be-hind; Speak, and God will hear it, For His heart is kind. Un-daunt-ed be; Morn-ing dawns for thee, And a new-er spring-time Breaks the froz-en sea. In ev-'ry tem-pest, And 'neath the rod, He will ev-er shield thee, Our gra-cious God.

2. Rouse thee, O my spir-it, Stay not be-hind, Speak, and God will hear it; For His heart is kind. When cour-age breaks, Heav-en ne'er for-sakes; Great-er than the need is He His kind-ness makes. Fa-ther e-ter-nal, Sav-iour in need, May we ev-er fol-low Where Thou dost lead.

HYMN OF PRAISE.

R. L. D. DELABORDE.

Moderato.
1. Come, let us praise the Lord And all His ma - ny won - ders, And let His fame re - sound Till earth and heav - en ring; From all in glad ac - cord A might - y cho - rus thun - ders, And all His host of an - gels sing,
cres.
2. Oh, won - der - ful the works Thy rul - ing will cre - at - ed; Thou, the Al - might - y, speakst, And all Thy word o - bey; The heav - ens, earth, and sea, Thy call to birth a - wait - ed, And o'er the void in beau - ty lay,
f
dim.
p
p

And all His host of an - gels sing.
cres.
dim.
And o'er the void in beau - ty lay.

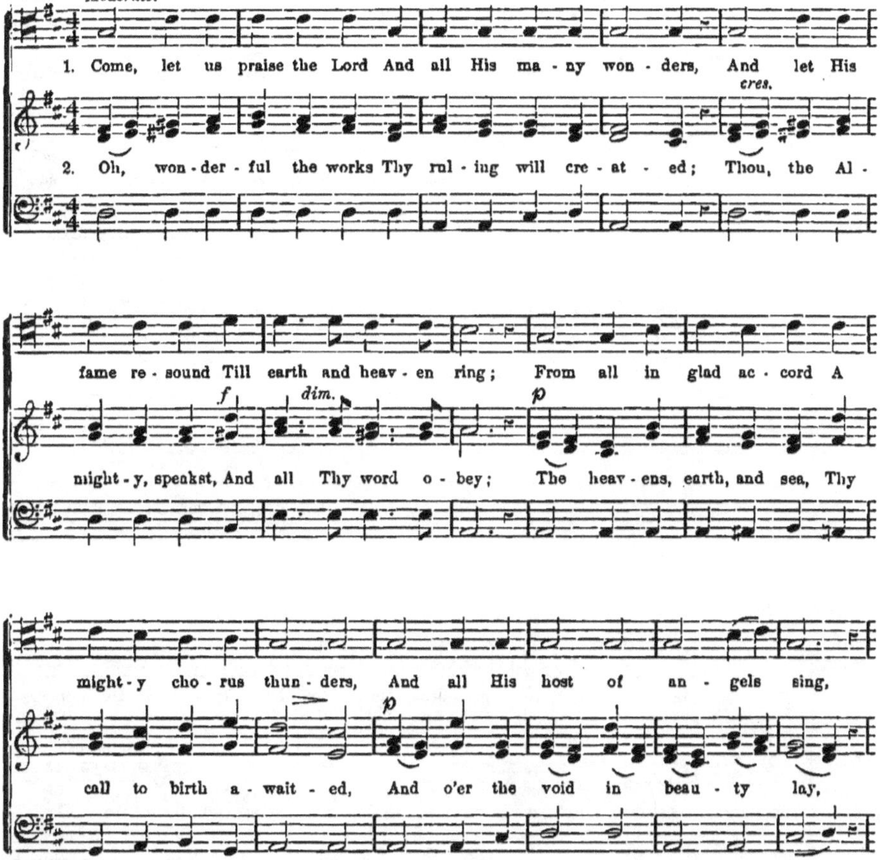

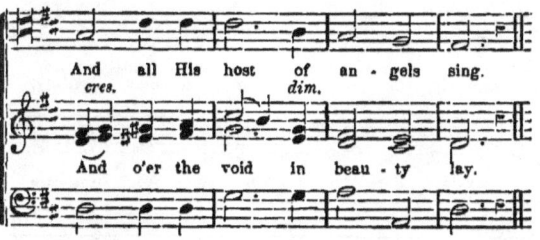

8.

The world and all therein
Shall fall at Thy commanding,
When Thou shalt come to judge
The people from Thy throne;
Yet, o'er the wreck, Thy truth
And right shall still be standing;
Unchanged art Thou and Thine alone

THE WAY OF PEACE.

R. L. D.
Andante.
KARL KLOSS (1792).

1. To dwell-ers in gloom there is peace, sweet peace; From toil may the wea-ry have glad re-lease;
2. Then here in the glow of the morn we raise Our voi-ces to heav-en in pray'r and praise;
3. In day-light and twi-light Thy hand we need, Our feet in the val-ley of peace to lead;

His nights and his days are un-known to fear, Who un-to the pres-ence of God is near.
As day is ad-vanc-ing in light, we ask Our strength to in-crease for each dai-ly task.
We jour-ney, dear Fa-ther, Thy face to see, May night nev-er find us a-stray from Thee.

WORSHIP.

R. L. D.
Moderato.
FRANZ ABT (1819—).

1. Fa-ther, in the heav'n-ly gar-dens, Hear Thy lov-ing chil-dren's pray'r;
2. Fa-ther, foun-tain of all mer-cy, Thou art ev-er our re-treat;
3. Fa-ther, take the songs we of-fer, Full of praise and thanks to Thee;

We con-fide in Thy great pow-er, When a-round us storm-clouds low-er,
They who cher-ish Thee most dear-ly, See the path of life most clear-ly,
Look up-on us now in pleas-ure, For Thy lov-ing smile we treas-ure,

3.
Lord, if e'er discord rises to-day,
May it be quickly driven away;
Help us to meet it with a bright smile,
Give us sweet concord, banishing guile.

4.
Living and dying, oh, may we be
Heavenward going, near unto Thee!
May gentle concord tarry till night,
Shedding its holy, heavenly light.

MORNING PRAISE.

TUNE—"*Song of Praise.*"

1 SUNLIGHT beams upon the earth,
  And the birds now praise Thy glory;
 Morning brings a newer birth,
  Life is all a pleasant story:
   Wake, O wake, my soul, and sing
   Praises to our heavenly King!

2 Blossoms fill the happy air
  With a perfume rich and tender;
 Brightest green the branches wear,
  Spring has come in youthful splendor:
   Wake, O wake, my soul, and sing
   Praises to our heavenly King!

3 Smiling faces meet my gaze,
  Full of hope and health unbounded;
 Youthful hearts are filled with praise,
  And by heaven's love surrounded:
   Wake, O wake, my soul, and sing
   Praises to our heavenly King!

THE UNKNOWN LAND.

W. Locke Smith.

2 We may not know how sweet its balmy air
 How bright and fair its flowers ;
We may not hear the songs that echo there
 Through those enchanted bowers.
The city's shining towers we may not see
 With our dim earthly vision ;
For death, the silent warden, keeps the key
 That opes those gates elysian.
  O land unknown, etc.

3 But sometimes, when adown the western sky,
 The fiery sunlight lingers,
Its golden gates swing inward, noiselessly,
 Unlocked by unseen fingers ;
And while they stand a moment, half ajar,
 Gleams from the inner glory,
Stream brightly through the azure vault afar,
 And half reveal the story.
  O land unknown, etc.

Words translated by R. L. D.
Andante.
From the German.

God liveth still! Soul, what fearest thou of ill? God is good, and from His kindness Sends His aid to all the earth; From His will and mighty power, Every blessing has its birth; While we fold our hands dejected, He brings triumph unexpected. Soul, be brave, and do not fear; God's protecting arm is near.

2. God liveth still! Soul, what fearest thou of ill? Is your life with burdens laden, Look to heaven then to-day; God is great, and rich in mercy, He will aid you on your way; His great love endures forever, He forsakes his children never, Soul, be brave, and do not fear; God's protecting arm is near.

3. God liveth still! Soul, what fearest thou of ill? Would you shun the world of evil, Think of evening's peaceful end; God will close His arms about you, And in troubles be your friend; Though the need may be unbounded, His great heart can ne'er be sounded. Soul, be brave, and do not fear; God's protecting arm is near.

ALMIGHTY RULER OF THE SKIES.

3 Oh, what are we, Thy love to share,
   Thy tender care to know!
  Yet Thou dost guard us, night and day,
   Wherever we may go!
  The silent, darksome watches through,
   Again Thy hand hath brought!
  And we would glorify Thy name
   In word and thought!

4 Oh, let our morning hymn to Thee
   As holy incense rise!
  And look in mercy, Lord, we pray,
   Upon us from the skies!
  Our wayward feet direct aright
   Until the close of day;
  And fill our hearts with love to Thee,
   While here we stay!

THE FAITHFUL GUIDE.

231

PRAISE AND THANKSGIVING.

C. F. RINCK (1770—1846).

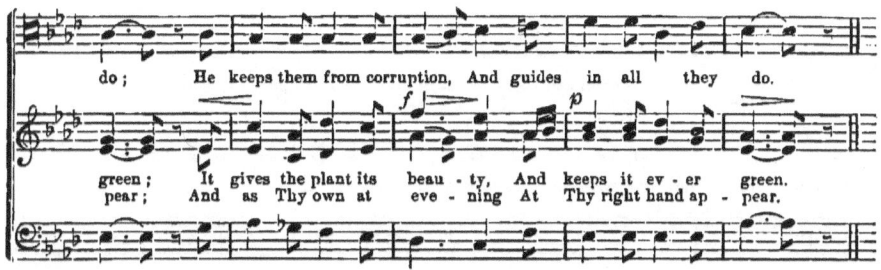

234 LET THE PEOPLE PRAISE THEE.

THE LOVE OF GOD. (Ave Verum.)

R. L. D.
W. A. Mozart (1756—1791).

THE LOVE OF GOD.

2.
Love, which is in death unending,
  Precious gift to my unworthy heart;
Gratefully before Thee bending,
  Oh, let me no more depart!
Lord, accept my humble treasure,
  Lest it spread a snare for me;
Be the Spirit's peace my pleasure,
  Take me lovingly to Thee!

IN MERCY REMEMBER.

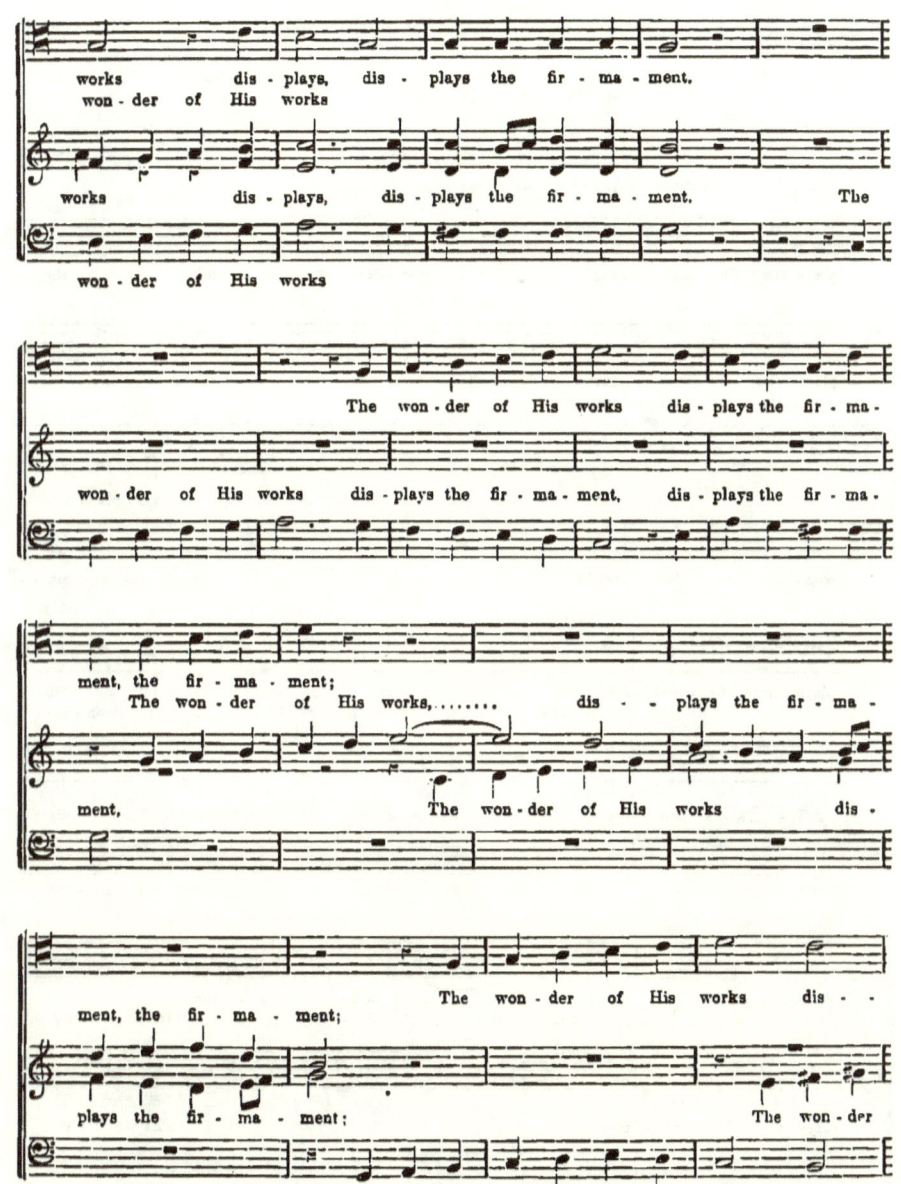

THE HEAVENS ARE TELLING.

LIFT UP YOUR HEADS.

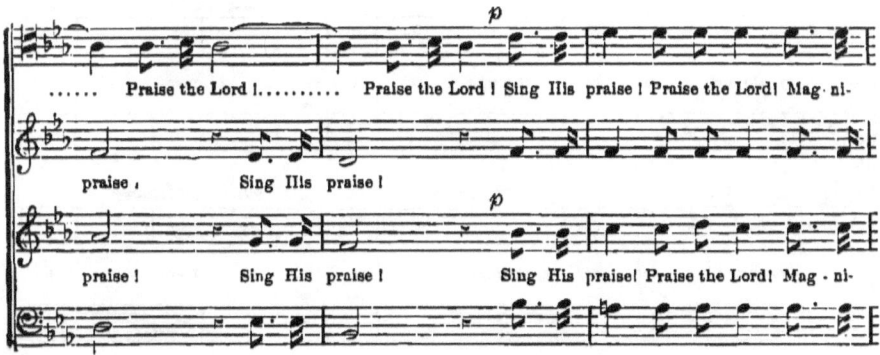

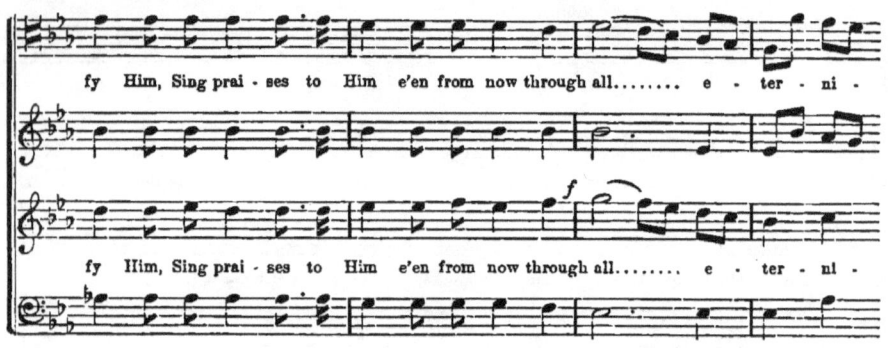

GLORIOUS IS THY NAME, O LORD.

GLORIOUS IS THY NAME, O LORD.

GLORIOUS IS THY NAME, O LORD.

INDEX.

	PAGE
Almighty Ruler	228
Alone	30
Alpine Shepherd's Song	130
Amelia	212
America	211
A Summer Picture	48
Awake! the Daylight falls	108
Ballad of the Weaver	158
Begone, dull Care	42
Be still in God	216
Blest Spring-time	124
But the Lord is mindful	30
But who may abide	40
Chants	215
Choral	229
Close of School	93
Come, come away	92
Come, gentle May	134
Coming of Spring	18
Come unto Him	40
Concord	223
Departure	70
Dream on	51
Early Morning	200
Early Spring	203
Echo Song	63
Evening	186
Evening Song	103
Eventide	219
Fair shines the Moon	148
Fairy Moonlight	89
Far down in yonder Vale	55
Fays and Elves	128
Forgive and Forget	127
Forth to the Battle	106
Glorious is Thy Name	251
God liveth still	227
Going a-Maying	65
Good Night	113, 132
Graduating Song	91
Hence, now away	120
Here we rest	82
He was despised	41
Holy Night	79
Home	154
Home Virtues	26
Hymn of the Fishermen's Children	84
Hymn of Praise	221
I know not	140
In Mercy Remember	236
In Summer-time	99
In the Glen	112
Italian Hymn	211
Land of Liberty	97
Let the People praise Thee	233
Lift up your Heads	246
Lightly tread	95
List ! the Trumpet's thrilling Sound	174
Lord, how great Thy Love	226
March of the Men of Harlech	144
May Day	103
Meditation	86
Mehul	210
Messiah	214
Morning Hymn	25
Morning Praise	217
Music on the Waves	44
Nature	97
Night, thou holy Night	188
Note the bright Hours	43
Oh, beautiful Dreams	142
Oh, the merry Harvest-time	152
Oh, 'tis merry	75
Old Friends and Old Times	50

	PAGE
Old Hundred	210
On the Mountains	156
Onward	147
Onward to Battle	75
Our Childhood's Days	109
Our Hearts are light	110
Over the Stars	218
Phœbus	166
Picnic Song	60
Praise	214
Praise and Thanksgiving	231
Protect us	206
Rouse thee, O my Spirit	220
Sabbath Eve	182
See how lightly	74
Serenade Song	163
Seymour	213
Signs of Spring	29
Silent Night	101
Song of Praise	224
Song of the Violet	73
Song of the Zephyr	180
Spring's bright Glances	68
Summer Song	77
Sweet and low	162
Sweet the Hour of Rest	125
The Angel of Patience	123
The Banner of the Free	169
The Chamois Hunter	136
The Chapel	177
The Curfew	64
The Dawning of the Day	194
The Earth is beautiful	167
The Evening Bell	46
The Faithful Guide	230
The Happy Peasants	84
The Heavens are telling	240
The Linden Tree	67
The Lord my Pasture	228
The Love of God	234
The May is here	27
The Nation's Cry	87
The Night	192
The Nightingale	190
The Ocean	47
The Old Familiar Place	94
The Old Man	183
The Primrose	189
The Quiet Eve	80
The Robin	88
The Sea	61
The Sea of Life	216
These Things can never die	107
The Spring's Awaking	117
The Sun smiles in Beauty	49
The Unknown Land	223
The Valley of Home	119
The Venetian Boatmen's Song	149
The Wanderer's Song	81
The Watch of the Stars	105
The Way of Peace	232
The Welcome Spring	137
Though we part	102
'Tis the Evening's holy Hour	202
'Tis the last Rose of Summer	102
To-day and To-morrow	83
Under the Blue	66
Vocal Waltz	116
Wandering in the May-time	52
We are Nymphs of the Ocean	53
Welcome, my Woods	178
Welcome to Spring	56
When Daylight faries away	96
When the Light of Memory	71
When the Loved Ones wait	138
Who with an honest Love	146
Work for the Night	218
Worship	229

www.ingramcontent.com/pod-product-compliance
Lightning Source LLC
Chambersburg PA
CBHW021401230426
43666CB00006B/599